Jo Whitehead is Assistant Director ... Youth Ministry, based at St John's C ... starting at St John's, Jo was Assistant N ... Nottinghamshire and worked with youn_ _ ,.. .ii cnurches, schools and communities. She was also a freelance writer, trainer and consultant. She has facilitated in a wide range of different denominational, educational, organizational and community contexts, and is currently undertaking doctoral research into whole-person learning and formation. Her other publications include *Inspire!*, *Inspire Too!*, *Youth Work After Christendom*, *Skills for Collaborative Ministry* and *An Introduction to Managing Yourself*. She is married and loves walking, gardening, cooking, visual journalling and various creative projects. Her website can be found at <www.wholelifelearning.co.uk>.

The Revd Dr Sally Nash is Director of the Midlands Centre for Youth Ministry based at St John's College Nottingham and is also Curate at Hodge Hill Church in Birmingham. Sally has exercised facilitation skills in a wide range of contexts. Her other publications include *Skills for Collaborative Ministry*, *Tools for Reflective Ministry*, *The Faith of Generation Y* and *Youth Ministry: A Multifaceted Approach*. She is currently researching shame in the church and spiritual care in a paediatric hospital context. She is a companion of the Northumbria Community, and a Trustee for Frontier Youth Trust and Youth for Christ. She blogs at <www.markerpostsandshelters.wordpress.com> and enjoys playing golf, tennis and walking by the sea.

The Revd Simon Sutcliffe is an ordained minister in the Methodist Church currently working part time as the tutor for evangelism and church growth at Queen's Foundation, Birmingham, and part time as a pioneer minister with Venture FX establishing new forms of Christian community in the Chester and Stoke-on-Trent District. He is part of a missional collective known as the Immerse Community – <www.ikidsgrove.wordpress.com> – and you can follow him on Twitter @urbanfriar. Simon's current research interest is in the future direction of ministry and ecclesiology, with particular reference to pioneer ministry and the worker priest movement. Simon has four children who help to keep him grounded.

SPCK Library of Ministry

Being a Chaplain
Miranda Threlfall-Holmes and Mark Newitt

Community and Ministry: An introduction to community
development in a Christian context
Paul Ballard and Lesley Husselbee

Developing in Ministry: A handbook for effective
Christian learning and training
Neil Evans

Facilitation Skills for Ministry
Jo Whitehead, Sally Nash and Simon Sutcliffe

Finding Your Leadership Style: A guide for ministers
Keith Lamdin

How to Make Great Appointments in the Church:
Calling, Competence and Chemistry
Claire Pedrick and Su Blanch

Pioneer Ministry and Fresh Expressions of Church
Angela Shier-Jones

Reader Ministry Explored
Cathy Rowling and Paula Gooder

Reflective Caring: Imaginative listening to pastoral experience
Bob Whorton

Skills for Collaborative Ministry
Sally Nash, Jo Pimlott and Paul Nash

Supporting Dying Children and their Families:
A handbook for Christian ministry
Paul Nash

Supporting New Ministers in the Local Church: A handbook
Keith Lamdin and David Tilley

Tools for Reflective Ministry
Sally Nash and Paul Nash

Transforming Preaching: The sermon as a channel for God's word
David Heywood

Youth Ministry: A multifaceted approach
Sally Nash

FACILITATION SKILLS FOR MINISTRY

SPCK Library of Ministry

JO WHITEHEAD,
SALLY NASH
and
SIMON SUTCLIFFE

First published in Great Britain in 2013

Society for Promoting Christian Knowledge
36 Causton Street
London SW1P 4ST
www.spckpublishing.co.uk

British Library Cataloguing-in-Publication Data
A catalogue record for this book is available from the British Library

ISBN 978–0–281–06877–7
eBook ISBN 978–0–281–06878–4

Typeset by Graphicraft Limited, Hong Kong
First printed in Great Britain by Ashford Colour Press
Subsequently digitally printed in Great Britain

eBook by Graphicraft Limited, Hong Kong

Produced on paper from sustainable forests

*This book is dedicated to all the groups
we have facilitated and continue to facilitate
within education, churches and our communities.*

Contents

Contents

Contents

Contents

Acknowledgements

I am grateful to all those who have been part of the journey of this book, especially to Sally and Simon for agreeing to partner in the project. So many people have lent encouragement and support. Particular thanks are due to Anne Topping and Mark Davis, who encouraged my early interest in facilitation processes, to my colleagues within the Centre for Youth Ministry and St John's College, to friends and family whose support and encouragement keep me going, to Tim and Sam who gave me space to write, and Philip Law at SPCK, whose enthusiasm led to a throwaway comment in a conversation developing into this publication. Many of my chapters were written sitting at a table in Anderson's in Breaston, Derbyshire, and I am grateful to Dean and Lynnette Anderson for their gift of creating hospitable spaces.

Last but certainly not least I would particularly like to thank my husband Paul, who read parts of the manuscript and whose insight and input on facilitating meetings was particularly helpful. His love, support, patience, encouragement and the steady stream of tea continue to be invaluable!

This book is dedicated to all the groups Sally, Simon and I have facilitated and continue to facilitate in churches, communities and within educational settings, with apologies for mistakes we have made along the way and gratitude for all the learning we have shared together.

Jo Whitehead

How to use this book

We are living in a highly participative culture. Most of us today are accustomed to having a say in decisions that will impact on us and issues that affect us. The days are largely gone when people would simply do as they were told because someone in authority said so. Society emphasizes consumer choice, individual freedom and personal power. Popular culture gives opportunity to shape television programmes through voting and give a running commentary on life through social media such as Twitter and Facebook.

Although trends within some sectors of the Church still focus around more hierarchical and authoritarian models of leadership, collaborative forms of ministry, team ministries and leadership teams are the norm and there is broad recognition that leadership authority needs to be shared, and leadership roles and responsibilities carried out by people with varying gifts and skills. Some of this reflects an embracing of the benefits of participation. For many traditional churches, however, declining numbers have necessitated increasing lay involvement, and new forms of church that have emerged in recent years, such as Fresh Expressions, are increasingly more participative in style. While consumerism is undeniably present within churches, in many contexts people appear to want to be involved in creating ministry themselves rather than in simply consuming it.

Many leaders are keen to adopt more participative approaches to leadership and to develop their facilitation skills for use in all kinds of different church and community settings. This book is designed to assist you in exploring how facilitative approaches might benefit your ministry practice, and to give practical suggestions in terms of developing your own facilitation skills.

We have sought to use a range of examples and illustrations from different contexts, but would encourage you, as you read, to contextualize the material, to make it appropriate for your setting, community and culture. The material focuses on working with groups, but many of the principles and suggestions can also be effectively used with individuals. Between us we operate and have continued to do so in a range of settings, including youth and community work, teaching, training, church leadership in new churches, traditional churches and pioneering contexts; two of us are ordained; all of us facilitate learning in higher education; and all of us are passionate about using facilitative processes to enable effectiveness and encourage the development and growth of those with whom we are working in all our various work and ministry contexts.

Styles and approaches to facilitation will vary from individual to individual and we are not seeking to prescribe one specific way to facilitate but rather to introduce a range of tools, methods, approaches and skills, which we would encourage you to use, adapt and personalize to fit with your context, personality, values and preferred ways of working.

The first six chapters address generic issues around facilitation and the last six consider some specific situations in which facilitation skills can be helpfully used. You can read the book straight through or dip in and out of different chapters, depending on your interest and situation. Inevitably there are potential overlaps between the issues covered in different chapters, and we have tried to avoid too much repetition by signposting where certain themes or issues are covered in more detail.

At the end of each chapter you will find suggestions for further action and reflection that can be used to help you develop your thinking or practice further. Alternatively, you could use these suggestions in a team or group context to structure reflection or training. There is a list of suggestions for further reading, arranged by chapter, towards the end of the book. Further practical resources, including various tools mentioned, can be found at <www.wholelifelearning.co.uk>. A Bibliography is provided to support the references in the text, but will in its own right give further pointers to reading around the subject.

Introduction and overview

JO WHITEHEAD

People support what they help create.   (Abraham Lincoln)

The word facilitation comes from the Latin word *facilis* ('easy'), and literally means 'to make easy' or 'to make simple'. When we facilitate we make things easy for people – or so the theory goes. Facilitation involves an approach to leadership that seeks to empower people to take responsibility for the decisions that affect them, be involved in processes, learn and participate. Facilitators provide frameworks by which and through which individuals and groups are enabled to work collaboratively towards their tasks or goals.

Although facilitators have been traditionally understood to have no official leadership role or decision-making power within the groups they work with (Schwarz, 2002), many of the skills involved in facilitation can be effectively used by people in a wide range of ministry contexts and with diverse roles and responsibilities. Facilitation skills, if used well, can enhance and develop leadership and encourage ownership and participation.

Styles of leadership

Most people have a preferred approach, or approaches to leadership. Your leadership style is likely to be influenced by your personality, preferences, upbringing, experience, training, key people who have influenced you, the culture of the organization, church or community you are working in and the expectations of those around you.

We can identify a spectrum of leadership styles, focused around the level of power and authority exercised by the leader and that given to or taken by the group.

Autocratic or Authoritarian

This style of leadership is dictatorial. Autocratic/authoritarian leaders make the decisions and those participating follow their lead. There

1

is usually very little participation from the group in decision-making processes. This style of leading can be seen as effective as it often results in things getting done, but it can easily become oppressive and repressive and it does not value or recognize the contribution individuals can make to organizations or churches.

Authoritative

This style also involves significant authority resting with the leader. Authoritative leaders will tend to be confident and assured, making clear decisions and taking action. However, there is usually some listening to others involved and people tend to feel freer to question decisions made and actions taken.

Consultative

This style is similar to an authoritative style, with a strong sense of decisive action, but leaders with a consultative approach tend to talk to others before making a final decision. They may speak to people involved or external experts or advisors. The level of input influencing the final decision will vary.

Participative

A participative style can encompass the consultative but is usually more clearly involving of others in the processes. Normally in a participative approach leaders and others are involved in decision-making together, even if the leader makes the final decision.

Democratic

A democratic approach involves everyone concerned in the process. The idea is that leaders and people work collaboratively to find the best way forward, and decisions are made democratically, usually by a vote or by consensus.

Laissez-faire

A laissez-faire approach is when leaders don't take an active or decisive lead but abdicate responsibility. This may be through lack of confidence, laziness, procrastination, a dislike of conflict or confrontation or through being overwhelmed by busyness or a sense of responsibility. Although a laissez-faire style tends to have quite negative connotations and consequences, occasionally a facilitator might choose this approach intentionally, to take a step back and encourage a group to take responsibility and 'manage itself' for a short time.

Chaotic

A chaotic style describes leadership that is disorganized, unstructured and provides little guidance or support. Leaders who operate like this have a tendency to move the goalposts depending on their mood or the situation. There is no consistency and little responsibility is taken, the leader tending to flit from a laissez-faire approach to authoritarian interventions when things go wrong.

Situational

In exploring leadership with various groups over the years I often find that individuals interpret the leadership style of Jesus through their own preferred paradigm. Those with a democratic or participative preference cite stories such as Jesus sending out the 72 (Luke 10.1–17), where the emphasis is on the disciples working together, taking responsibility and being empowered to minister. Those whose style is more naturally authoritative will cite instances where Jesus appears to eschew participation in favour of being more commanding and assertive (see, for example, the calming of the storm in Luke 8.22–25 or the healing of the demon-possessed man in Luke 8.26–33). In fact it appears that Jesus led situationally, adopting the approach that was most appropriate to each given situation.

Similarly, I would suggest that effective facilitators will utilize a number of the approaches above to work with people in a group context. So, for example, you will need to take a strong lead to give a group confidence, set and maintain boundaries, challenge inappropriate, bullying or discriminatory behaviour or attitudes and actively delegate roles and responsibilities. At other times, particularly when a group is functioning effectively, you may choose to step back and allow the group autonomy, being present and contributing where appropriate but taking little authoritative role in the conversation, discussion or process.

Those with a purist approach to facilitation would insist that a facilitative style should always be situated at the participative-democratic end of the spectrum, arguing that facilitation, by definition, is egalitarian. We would want to take a more pragmatic approach and suggest that all leaders, whatever their preferred style, can benefit from using facilitative approaches. Indeed, we hope that the suggestions given in this book will help leaders at both ends of the spectrum to integrate more participation, ownership, collaboration and empowerment into their ministry practice. Almost anyone can use facilitation skills to enhance their practice, and this can create valuable space for others to express themselves and their opinions, grow in confidence and see a sense of community engendered.

Participation

A facilitative approach in a ministry context is about empowering God's people to participate; it involves recognizing that everyone has something to give and finding ways to help them bring what they have. Use of power within facilitation is understood to be power 'with' as opposed to 'power over': 'Effective facilitation encourages each person to value, develop and express their full sense of self, and be in authentic relationship with others individually and as part of a group working towards collective goals' (Hunter et al., 2007:21). In this sense participation fosters a culture that encourages people to develop and take responsibility rather than one that encourages dependence on leaders.

There are all kinds of reasons why leaders find it difficult to adopt a participative approach. Yasmina described a session at a conference that had been facilitated rather than taught more traditionally. In this context she reflected with a sense of frustration that it felt as if everyone present was simply pooling their ignorance. Chris shared his concern that adopting a facilitative approach in his context might result in power struggles, particular individuals within the group seeking to take over or dominate. In my experience, good preparation and honed skills can mitigate some of the potential difficulties that might result from using facilitative approaches.

The ladder of participation (adapted from Hart, 1992) identifies a number of different levels of participation and shows how you might seek to increase levels of participation in your setting (see Figure 1). It is important to note that the first three rungs of the ladder are not really genuine participation at all, and I would want to stress at this point that facilitative approaches should not be used as a way of playing at participation, using tokenism, decoration or manipulation to mask a highly authoritarian approach.

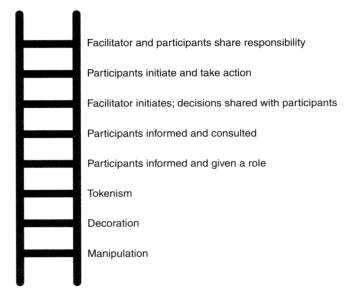

Facilitator and participants share responsibility

Participants initiate and take action

Facilitator initiates; decisions shared with participants

Participants informed and consulted

Participants informed and given a role

Tokenism

Decoration

Manipulation

Figure 1 Ladder of participation

Encouraging participation is not always as straightforward as it might at first appear. Groups or individuals can be reluctant to take responsibility because of past experience, preconceived ideas of what the group is about, fears about what people might think, low self-esteem, apathy, boredom, unhealthy group dynamics or simply the mood or level of motivation prevailing. Particularly where a strongly authoritarian style is the norm, adopting a facilitative approach may feel uncomfortable and even threatening for group members. Where people are unused to participating actively it is important to consider how you might provide assistance to increase levels of involvement gradually and move people further 'up the ladder', developing the confidence of individuals and the group as a whole.

Different needs in facilitation

One model that is helpful as we consider facilitation in its broadest sense is John Adair's model of group needs (adapted from Adair and Thomas, 2004) – see Figure 2, overleaf. He identifies three areas of need:

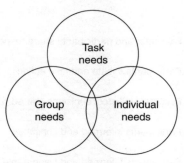

Figure 2 Group needs

1 *Achieving the task* – aspects that relate to the task or goals of the group.
2 *Motivating and developing the individual* – aspects relating to the well-being, participation and growth of individuals within the group.
3 *Building and maintaining the group or team* – aspects that assist in developing a sense of community within the group and enhancing the experience of working as a group together.

Effective facilitation will focus on all three of these and will find ways of maintaining a helpful and healthy balance between them, while recognizing that at times more emphasis might be needed in one particular area. Being aware of your own preference for a task or relationship (group and individual) emphasis will assist you in ensuring that you spend time focusing on those aspects that don't necessarily come naturally to you.

In seeking to balance these three areas of need you will find yourself adopting a number of different roles within the process. Certain of these roles will fit with specific needs of the group and can be best understood in the light of these. Task-oriented roles would include: leader, planner, administrator, initiator, information provider, stirrer and evaluator. More relationally oriented roles would include process designer, leader, host, boundary-keeper, mediator, encourager and pastor.

Five dimensions of facilitation

My approach to facilitation is structured around understanding five essential dimensions of purpose, product, process, people and place

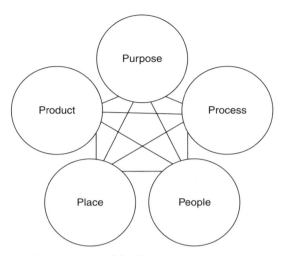

Figure 3 Five dimensions of facilitation

(see Figure 3). The word dimension is deliberately chosen here to encompass not only the sense of an aspect or characteristic but something that can be measured and planned for. These dimensions are not completely separate but intersect and influence each other. They will be explored in different ways and in more depth throughout this book.

Purpose

The purpose is the *why* of facilitation. In any context where we might use facilitation skills, it is essential to have a clear understanding of what we are seeking to do. A sense of purpose encompasses where we are heading and what we are hoping to accomplish. This might be held lightly as a background to our thinking or framed formally in terms of aims, goals or objectives. Our purpose will give us the sense of direction we need, not only to plan what we are trying to do but to help us know if and when we achieve it. Purposes can be multifaceted: we may have one clear purpose or a number of different ones. Our purpose may be part of a longer-term plan or a bigger picture, the wider scope of which we may need to bear in mind as we undertake our own part in the process.

Although in some cases our purpose might be hidden from those who are participating, experience and good practice would suggest that things work best when participants clearly understand why they are there and what the purpose of the meeting, session or process is. When our purposes are specific, explicit and clearly communicated, those involved are enabled to have a sense of ownership of what is going on, which in turn can increase their motivation, enthusiasm and sense of responsibility.

Product

The product is the *what* of facilitation. This is very closely linked to the purpose in that it comprises what we hope will emerge or result from the facilitated experience. In management language, products are described in terms of outcomes or outputs – literally, what comes out in the end. Some of these outcomes will be clear and easy to measure – a decision made, something clearly learnt, a way forward agreed, an issue resolved. Other outcomes – personal learning, change and growth, the developing of relationships, community and collaborative working – may be equally important but much more difficult to measure.

Identifying intended outcomes will help you measure the effectiveness of what you do – to gauge whether you have achieved or partly achieved what you set out to accomplish. A word of caution is important here. Those of us who are more task-oriented may find ourselves focusing too much on product, to the detriment of other parts of the process. It is important that this does not become a 'tick box' exercise that helps us justify what we are doing but rather serves as a way of keeping the end in sight, maintaining focus and direction and measuring effectiveness.

Process

Process is the *how* of facilitation. If purpose and product focus on the destination, the process is about the way we will get to where we want to go. A significant aspect of the facilitator's role is that of process designer (Knowles et al., 1973). Designing process is a bit like planning a journey and thinking about the specific route that we might take, the forms of transport that might work best, where we might stop off and for what purpose, what equipment and sustenance we might need along the way. Effective facilitators will give as much consideration to how they are going to get somewhere as to where they are going. This involves careful consideration of tools and approaches, congruence between purpose and methodology, creativity and variety, levels of interaction and participation, information, resources and roles.

One aspect of process design involves thinking about the extent to which we will map out the process in advance and the extent to which we will involve participants in the process design. If we take the journey metaphor again, some people will prefer to plan a journey intricately, going into huge detail and preparing for every possible contingency. Others will prefer to take a more exploratory approach, allowing space and time to enjoy the scenery, look around a bit and go off on a few detours. Our approach to process design will inevitably be influenced by our personal preferences and our context, but our purpose and intended product should influence and inform the way we design processes for particular situations.

People

The people are the *who* of facilitation. Those involved will create a dynamic unique to each context. In one-to-one situations this dynamic is relatively straightforward, but group work encompasses a whole web of relationships that emerges as we work with individuals and the group as a whole. As facilitators our relationships with individuals will be influenced and affected by the different contexts in which we know people, prior experiences, preconceived ideas and expectations both ways. The relationships within the group will bring further complexity – the network of the known and the unknown, different personalities and preferences, potential conflicts, tensions and projections, history, experience and expectations will all contribute. Our relationship with the group as a whole will be influenced by all these factors – we will be aware of some of them and oblivious of others.

Ringer suggests that a key factor in the effective facilitation of group work is that the leader is 'fully present' at every moment and providing appropriate support (2002:18). This is more than simply a physical presence, rather one that has a dynamic quality to it. Your own sense of identity and the way you influence the group and use power, your security, integrity, congruence and self-awareness will be significant here.

Place

Place is about the *where* of facilitation. This will involve consideration of the physical space and practicalities associated with this. Where we meet and how we use the space will influence people's participation and experience. A sense of place also encompasses issues around the emotional, social and spiritual climate of the one-to-one or the group, and we will need to consider how we create a safe – although not always comfortable – space through boundaries and contracting.

The Spirit as facilitator

Elsewhere I have begun to explore the Spirit as a metaphor for facilitation (Nash et al., 2008:44–5), and I find this provides a helpful focus in developing understanding of facilitative processes. The Spirit is described in the Gospel of John (14.16, 26; 15.26; 16.7) as the *paraclete* or 'one who comes alongside' (Vine, 1985:208). That sense of accompanying is a useful one for facilitators, whose role often encompasses being with, presence and solidarity.

In the New Testament, the Spirit is seen as one who speaks (1 Timothy 4.1), opens understanding (1 Corinthians 2.12), leads into truth (1 John 2.27), teaches (John 16.13), enables (John 4.23–24; Romans 8.26–28) and empowers (Acts 1.8). However, the Spirit does not appear to override the will of the individual, who can resist, quench, grieve or respond to the Spirit. This is highlighted, for example, in 1 Corinthians 14.32, which makes it clear that in that particular church those with prophetic gifts can choose to speak or remain silent. This sense of individual free will is vitally important when it comes to understanding our role.

Another important aspect when considering Spirit as a metaphor for facilitation is the sense in which mystery plays a significant role. There is something unknowable about the nature of the Spirit, whose ways of working are not easily defined or explained (see, for example, John 3.8). We can learn, develop and improve our facilitation skills but there is a sense of the unknown at the heart of the process, which makes it stimulating, perplexing, challenging and exhilarating. Even the most experienced facilitators will constantly find themselves in new situations and facing fresh challenges. Our ability to respond to what emerges from the group may develop, but the multitude of diverse factors involved in the dynamics of working with people individually and in groups means that the processes cannot necessarily be easily understood, ordered or controlled. This can be challenging for those of us who like things to be planned, organized and highly structured.

Embracing facilitative approaches therefore invites us to rediscover a childlike attitude to learning, living and leading. It invites us to take risks and learn afresh, and requires us to develop a dependency on God for wisdom, discernment and courage as we step out into the unknown.

For action and reflection

- Consider the spectrum of leadership styles. Which styles resonate most with you in terms of describing your preferred or normal ways of working? Give some thought as to how and why you developed this style – as a result of your context, role models, your values, skills, experience?
- Think about a situation recently when you have either facilitated a session or been in a session facilitated by someone else. Seek to identify how the five dimensions of facilitation outlined here influenced and informed the process. Jot these down or map them out in a chart or diagram.
- Do you tend to have a task- or relationship-focus when it comes to facilitation? Which roles do you tend to adopt? How could you actively develop roles that you normally don't use?
- How do you respond to the metaphor of the Spirit as facilitator? What other metaphors could you use that would assist you in your understanding of facilitation?

1

Values and attributes of effective facilitators

SALLY NASH

Treat people as if they were what they ought to be and you help
them to become what they are capable of being.   (Goethe)

Most of us will have experienced being in groups facilitated by people
who make us feel inadequate, foolish, bored or who bring out the
naughty child in us. However, hopefully we also will have been in
settings where we have been filled with wonder, achievement, joy and
that sense of becoming more who God created us to be. Significant
indicators of whether we experience the former or the latter are the
values and attributes of the facilitator.

Before exploring both values and attributes in more detail, I want
to suggest that underpinning everything that a facilitator does should
be the notion of servanthood. This draws again on an understanding
of facilitation as 'to render easier' (Brockbank and McGill, 1998:145),
which is often the role of a servant. Can you imagine the surprise
of the disciples at the last supper when Jesus takes on the role of the
lowliest of servants and washes their feet? John's Gospel then recounts
how Jesus returned to the table and encouraged his disciples to follow
the example that he had set, that of being a servant (13.15). Seeing
facilitation as servanthood is a good starting place for exploring the
role – one that is important to communicate to others. Often facilitation is about ensuring that others accomplish what they have come
to do either individually or as a group, and this may well mean putting
aside your own preferences or needs as you seek to facilitate others
in the way that will bring the best out of them.

The author of the letter to the church at Colossae advocates that
'As God's chosen ones, holy and beloved, clothe yourselves with compassion, kindness, humility, meekness, and patience' (Colossians 3.12,

NRSV). This notion of clothing ourselves is one that is valuable in reflecting on ourselves as facilitators. We can all instantly recall situations where clothing ourselves with patience seemed an imperative, but as you read this chapter you may want to reflect on which values and attributes it would be helpful to clothe yourself with, or at least have a basketful of different 'clothes' that you know you can draw on. Malcolm Gladwell (2008) suggests that 10,000 hours of practice leads to expertise and success in an area. While many of us may not spend that much time facilitating others, there are values and attributes that will contribute to our becoming effective.

Values

Our values can be seen as our ethical ideals, those things that motivate and inspire us, that shape what we do and how we do it and what we seek to achieve. Our values are both shaped by who we are and what we have experienced, and shape who we are becoming. For example, Natalie experienced some prejudice against both her youth and gender early on in ministry, and in her facilitation of groups it is clear that she puts a high value on hearing from everyone and not allowing people to dominate. This could be seen as valuing **equality**. Below are some of the values I believe enrich facilitation and that will help you draw out the best in those you are facilitating.

Perhaps the most important value in a facilitator is to believe that adopting a facilitative approach is appropriate and relevant in this context. If you don't believe in what you are doing then it is hard to get those you are facilitating to buy into the process. This can sometimes happen when we are given a task to do with which we don't agree or for which we have not been properly briefed or prepared. If this is ever the case then it is particularly important that the values we communicate to participants are life giving. Two other more general values are **mutuality** and **hospitality**. As a facilitator it is helpful to acknowledge that we learn from the participants, not just that they learn from us – there is a mutual exchange rather than it just being one-way. Understanding facilitation as hospitality is also a significant value that can change our attitude towards what we are trying to do. Megan was impressed as she watched the external facilitator for a church consultation welcome everyone, get to know their names and help create a hospitable space out of a church hall that was unfamiliar to most attending.

13

Values towards participants

Affirming the uniqueness and worth of each individual as those made in the image of God (Genesis 1.27) with gifts, abilities and experiences to contribute is a value that underpins many of the others. It can be important actually to communicate this to the group rather than assume people know it. Closely allied to this is **respect**, particularly giving equal respect to each person. Sadly, in church contexts there is sometimes a hierarchy of respect, and deference is given to particular people, which can lead to some individuals or groups feeling as if their voice or contribution does not matter. This leads to another value, that of **inclusivity**. When asked to facilitate any group or when drawing a group together to explore an issue, a significant question to ask is: 'Who, if anyone or any group of people, has been excluded and why?' If you are not happy with the answer then perhaps the make-up of the group needs revisiting.

Associated with this is **valuing diversity** and facilitating with this in mind, and with its being a genuine valuation, as opposed to paying lip-service to a concept often discussed but not always honoured in practice.

Another set of values that are helpful to adopt towards participants are around being **accepting, encouraging** and **supportive**. Beyond these basic values of working with people in groups we can also consider the importance of being **loving, caring, compassionate** and **empathetic,** and how we manifest these values in our facilitation. Some find helpful the idea of **unconditional positive regard**, a concept developed by Carl Rogers (1961), in encapsulating how we should view those with whom we work.

Considering this list of values, one way to summarize it could be what is known as the **Golden Rule**: 'In everything, do to others what you would have them do to you' (Matthew 7.12). That can be a good starting point in thinking about values for facilitation, as long as this is seen conceptually rather than literally – our personality will partly dictate how we want people to treat us.

Personal values

As well as a range of values that facilitators hold towards participants, there are personal values that can help make facilitation more effective. Being **Christ-centred** helps in trying to ensure that facilitation is not about our own insecurities or needs. As Philippians 2.5 (NEB) says, 'Let your bearing towards one another arise out of your life in Christ Jesus'. Other values that flow out of this focus on being Christ-centred are **integrity, perseverance, accountability** and **loyalty**. As facilitators our integrity is important – we need to try to engender trust in others, and this is difficult if we are not demonstrating that we are trustworthy. One of the values that Jesus models is perseverance. There are times in facilitation where there is a temptation to give up or take the easy route rather than work through some of the difficulties and complexities that arise when working with people.

Another context where perseverance is important is when we are being misunderstood, and in some settings a **liberative** and **empowering** facilitator may be unfamiliar and be offering a model of leading with which some are uncomfortable. Accountability and loyalty can be quite complex issues in facilitation because they can often lie in several places. We should feel an accountability and loyalty to those who lead, and groups we are facilitating are not places in which to collude with others against a leadership that we might be part of, for example. However, we will also feel a sense of accountability and loyalty to participants to enable them to gain the most from the experience. However, we need to work out, in advance, possibly, what some of the boundaries are and agree ground rules with the group concerning such matters as confidentiality. These issues will be discussed in greater detail in Chapter 3.

Attributes of effective facilitators

Who the facilitator is will be a significant factor in his or her effectiveness, and understanding some of our weaknesses and limitations can help us see where we might be vulnerable and what we need to work towards. Hunter et al. suggest that in each moment we 'have a choice to expand – give – contribute – appreciate – live or to contract – take – pull back – criticize – die' (2007:50). As facilitators we have this choice and need to be aware of our own tendencies. We also need to be aware that those we are facilitating have these choices too, and the way we facilitate may contribute to the choices they make at different times. 'By their fruit you will recognise them' (Matthew 7.16) is an apt verse to introduce the attributes of effective facilitators. Skilled facilitation can appear almost effortless, but that is often far from the case: it is derived from years of practice and development. In this section I will explore some of the most important attributes for facilitators to develop.

Self-awareness

Knowing who we are and what we bring to facilitation (reflexivity) is vital. Who or what do people see when we walk into a room, and to what extent have we created an image to shape this? Some areas to reflect on include:

- Clothes, accessories and appearance.
- Language – what is the right register for this context?
- What does my body language communicate – open, defensive, nervous and so on?
- Do I have gestures or phrases that are distracting or irritating? You know what I mean!
- Do I need to reflect on touch? How do I use touch? What is suitable in different contexts?
- How do I use eye contact?
- Technology and communication styles: Prezi and PowerPoint communicate different things.

It is important to become conscious of what you do and the impact this has on others. Although painful for many of us it can be really helpful to watch a video of ourselves facilitating since that can provide insights in many of these areas. Do not forget your online presence. If you are an external facilitator or new into a context, participants may well have done an internet search on you. What will they find and how might this impact on them before they have even met you in person?

At a deeper level it is imperative to be aware of our own negative feelings and reactions – these can be destructive in a facilitation context if they arise unexpectedly and we are relatively unaware of them.

Widdicombe (1994:44) suggests four questions that are helpful to consider in relation to this:

1 What do I find most difficult when coping with emotions of . . . or towards . . . or aroused by . . . ?

2 What are the feelings this arouses in me?

3 What would help me to control my emotions and use them positively?

4 What can I learn from this?

As Hunter et al. note, 'the most important work for any facilitator is developing one's own capacity to be and become an embodied, grounded, self-aware and self-reflecting person – to facilitate yourself' (2007:46). They identify some questions that may be helpful in working towards this: Are you comfortable with yourself the way you are right now? Your body, feelings, thoughts, gender and sexual orientation, your cultural and national affinities? They suggest that many of us are not – and that we expend a lot of energy hoping that people will not find this out – but that we need to work on self-acceptance, growing and developing rather than any notion of trying to fix ourselves, because this starts with an assumption that there is something wrong with us.

Being aware of the issues in facilitating yourself will help you in facilitating others. The facilitator will often set the tone and the culture in a context and if they are not comfortable in who they are this may well be picked up by at least some of those being facilitated. While we may never be perfect, working towards accepting who we are with our weaknesses and limitations, while being committed to becoming more whole, can be a place where we are comfortable with who we are but perhaps not fully satisfied, which gives scope for us to continue to be conformed into the image of Christ (Romans 8.29). Being secure in who we are cannot be underestimated as a vital quality for effective facilitators.

Self-disclosure

One of the attributes of an effective facilitator is appropriate self-disclosure. This needs to be thought through and modelled well to enable group members both to feel safe within the group and be willing to disclose themselves. Jenny was in a training session on her gap year when a visiting speaker unknown to the group began sharing about problems of being attracted to a staff member of the opposite sex (the speaker was married). The atmosphere in the room changed and became quite hostile, since this was seen as inappropriate disclosure in the context. This is not to say that the issue is not real or important but the facilitator of that session had not built a relationship with the group where such disclosures could be heard and reflected on and lessons learnt. Some of the things to consider around self-disclosure include when and where we do this, whether within the formal context or not; the breadth and depth of what we want to share; the proportion of time or frequency given to this; and what the purpose or intended outcome of the disclosure is. If the facilitator is the person who discloses first then that sets the tone for everyone else within the group and helps to overcome some of the barriers people feel in contexts where they are encouraged to share something personal about themselves.

While self-disclosure should normally be purposeful, we need to be aware that there is some self-disclosure that we cannot avoid and that may lead people to draw conclusions about us – with varying degrees of accuracy. Thus things such as our size, shape, speech patterns, home, car, watch, handbag, tattoos, piercings, shoes, even which version of the Bible we use, may all be seen as disclosing something about who we are. While some of these areas are a matter of our personal choice, we may not have made the choice in the light of what this may disclose to others about us. We may also inadvertently or accidentally self-disclose in unexpected ways when something surprising or unforeseen happens or when overheard or seen in a context different from the one in which an individual knows us. When facilitating, it can be helpful to have considered the potential impact of these different areas.

Further important attributes

There is a range of attributes that are helpful in life generally but particularly valuable when facilitating. **Resilience**, which helps us cope with stress and adversity, is a quality to develop. Without resilience it is easy to get discouraged when things go wrong or to self-blame and bear burdens that are not ours to bear. Connected with this is **patience**. Effective facilitation can take time, both in relation to our own skills but also in specific contexts. Sometimes we need to go at the pace of the slowest person in the group if we want to build consensus and enable everyone to come to a decision or opinion with which they are genuinely content. **Flexibility** and **adaptability** are vital even if you are normally the most careful planner.

Jack arrived at church to lead a meeting and was planning to start with an upbeat devotion, but was greeted with the news that a much-loved member of the congregation had died earlier that day. He quickly substituted Psalm 23 for what he had planned. While some of this book is written in a way that talks about an individual facilitator, the task is often more **collaborative**, even if the actual task of facilitation is taken by one person. Often significant discussion will have taken place before the event and will need to occur afterwards, and a collaborative, team-enhancing approach and attitude will often be much more suitable than the lone-ranger approach. Being **courageous**, a term that might be a little more helpful than risk-taking when working with people, is the final core attribute I want to highlight.

Process attributes

Attributes of an effective facilitator in relation to the process of facilitation include:

- developing a hospitable atmosphere and safe space where people listen to each other (this will be explored more fully in Chapter 3);
- valuing all contributions and asserting an egalitarian approach where each person's contribution has an equal right to be heard;
- encouraging discussion and consideration of a wide range of views, being careful to use non-judgemental language but also working towards identifying criteria that will help achieve an outcome;
- being non-directive – asking questions rather than making statements;
- being comfortable with silence – you are not there to fill the gaps, and allowing times of silence can reduce dependency on the facilitator;
- helping people tap into their imagination or memory – try starting sentences with imagine, remember, think about, reflect on, consider . . .;
- being sensitive and responsive to the pace of the gathering or session and the need for breaks, energizers and so on;
- being willing to evaluate the process and your role within it.

A skilled facilitator will also have the attribute of helping people process their emotions. Kline writes powerfully, saying that

All around you every day are people whose churned-up, built-up feelings are blocking their thinking. But for some reason we make them stuff all those feelings back inside on pain of social death and then expect them to think and perform like geniuses. Even though, day after day, we can see right in our faces that this does not work, we do it over and over again. (1999:75)

This is where some of the creative approaches discussed in Chapter 5 may be useful, as well as using breaks to engage one to one with some people where this is needed. However, it can be important to name emotions that are there beneath the surface since often if one person is feeling it then others may be too, and if we are in the grip of a powerful emotion, it can be hard to think and fully contribute to an activity.

Power

Effective facilitators need to be aware that they carry power whether they like it or not, and need to be comfortable with power, aware that it exists in different ways and willing to share it. It is naive in the extreme to think that as a facilitator you can have no power, but others have power too, and the way in which different power interacts within the group can have a significant impact on process. Beasley-Murray (1998) discusses a range of approaches to power. As a facilitator you will probably be seen as having both legitimate and expert power and probably also information power. However, within the group there are possibly others with information power, and you can encourage them to use this positively and helpfully as part of the process. In many cases there may be connection power where individuals or groups have a particular relationship with those who have power within the organization. It is helpful to take this into account. There may also be referent power where, because they are liked and respected, one or more individuals are perceived by others as having power outside of the legitimate structures. They may be informal leaders or peer leaders, and if you win them over others are likely to follow. Coercive power is always inappropriate in a facilitation context – sanctions or punishment should not be part of a facilitator's toolkit!

Fruit and gifts of the Holy Spirit

We have explored a variety of different values and attributes of effective facilitators, but it would be remiss not to identify the fruit and gifts of the Holy Spirit as offering biblical examples of what these should be. The theological dimensions of the Holy Spirit as facilitator have been discussed in the Introduction, but asking God for the gifts and fruit of the Spirit that will be needed in the specific context is an integral part of being effective. As Galatians 5.22–23 states: 'the fruit of the Spirit is love, joy, peace, forbearance, kindness, goodness, faithfulness, gentleness and self-control'.

For action and reflection

- Are there any other values and attributes that you think are important in facilitation?
- Which values and attributes are your strengths as a facilitator? How can you build on them?
- Consider who the most skilled facilitators you know are. Spend some time reflecting on the values and qualities you see in them. What can you learn from them?
- Ask someone to video you facilitating a group – watch it back and seek to assess yourself objectively. How do you come across? What non-verbal messages do you communicate?

2

Basic facilitation skills

JO WHITEHEAD

> The role of the facilitator offers an opportunity to dance with
> life on the edge of a sword – to be present and aware – to be
> with and for people in a way that cuts through to what enhances
> life. A facilitator is a peaceful warrior.   (Dale Hunter)

Developing our facilitation skills is an ongoing and never-ending process. There is always more to learn. Skills are abilities that can be learnt, developed and honed. Thompson (2002) highlights the danger of mistaking skills for qualities or characteristics and suggests that this can limit our progress and development because we don't see ourselves as a particular 'sort of person'. Some people appear to facilitate effortlessly. Others seem to facilitate out of their personality but I believe it is crucial to understand and develop our skills, however charismatic (or not) we may be, so that we can grow ourselves and assist others in developing their skills and abilities. The apostle Paul appears to go to great lengths to persevere in becoming all he can be for the sake of the gospel. He speaks of the rigours of training and toughening himself up with discipline (1 Corinthians 9.25–27) and emphasizes the importance of pressing on with perseverance (Philippians 3.15).

Planning skills

For many leaders planning is something that we do tacitly without really thinking through the processes we use, but it is helpful to take a step back and seek to improve the way we plan and prepare.

Sandy Adirondack (1998:62) identifies seven different kinds of planning:

1 strategic planning – long term with a broad overview;
2 action planning – steps to implement a strategic plan;

3 cyclical planning – for regular events or activities;
4 project planning – for a specific, time-limited piece of work;
5 operational planning – to keep the organization or team running smoothly;
6 day-to-day planning – specific actions that need to be done immediately;
7 contingency planning – planning for the unforeseen.

As facilitators we may find ourselves involved in all these different kinds of planning at different times. We can see planning as a process with different stages:

- confirming overall aim or vision;
- assessing needs;
- setting aims;
- setting objectives;
- process planning;
- implementation;
- evaluation.

This is not a straight line but rather a cyclical process, and the reality is nowhere near as straightforward or linear as this list would imply. You may find things cropping up that mean you need to reassess needs or evaluate at different points. Similarly, changes in a group or situation may mean you need to look again at your aims or seek to implement them differently. However, it is important not to neglect any of these stages, and mapping them out in this way helps to consider the importance of each in turn.

Overall vision

Before beginning to plan it is important to ensure that you are clear about what your overall vision and purpose is. If you are working within a church or organization, your planning should reflect its overall vision and aims. This aspect of the planning cycle relates to the purpose of the gathering you intend to facilitate – the *why* aspects of what we are doing.

Needs analysis

Once you have a clearly established overall vision and purpose, it is important to consider the needs of the group, individuals and/or task you are working with. The types of needs you will explore and identify will be influenced by the situation and the context. You may need to consider a broader range of stakeholders as well as people who will be directly involved in the group.

Setting aims and objectives

Identifying needs gives a platform from which to set aims and objectives – these relate to the product dimension of facilitation and summarize your hoped-for outcomes. An aim is a general statement that summarizes in broad terms what you are seeking to do. Once aims have been agreed they can be broken down into smaller, manageable chunks – your objectives. An objective is a description of an intended outcome written in specific terms. Good objectives will be SMART:

Specific – so that you know exactly what to do.
Measurable – so you will know when you get there or when you have done it.
Achievable – so you know it is possible to achieve with the time and resources available.
Realistic – so you know it is practically possible and not simply fantasy.
Time-bounded – so you know by when you are aiming to accomplish it.

Process planning

Once agreed, objectives provide a helpful focus and framework to structure a process for facilitation. This aspect of the cycle includes consideration of the methodologies you will use, in other words the approaches, activities, input, order and style. This will vary depending on your context, and suggestions are given in future chapters as to how you might go about designing effective processes. It is also important to think at this point about the dimensions of people and place and plan accordingly in regard to those. Again, this will be covered in more depth later.

Implementation

Implementing your plans is the most visible part of the planning cycle and it is often only in the outworking of the plans – the actual 'doing' of the work – that we discover how effective our planning has been. You cannot plan for every eventuality, but thinking through the practical implications of what you intend to do can help ensure that things run smoothly. Having a written plan for a session, a project or a programme is likely to prove helpful. Also consider planning contingencies for things that may go wrong. This may be particularly helpful when you don't know the context or, for example, are not sure how many people are likely to be involved.

Evaluation

Evaluation is about making assessments of how things are going and how things have gone. You can undertake **formative** evaluation while things are going on in order to inform how you proceed, or **summative** evaluation, which involves assessing a project, session, activity or group at the end. We will consider this in more detail in Chapter 7 but it is important to note that your evaluation is likely to feed back into the planning cycle as needs are highlighted and issues raised.

Collaborative planning

Planning can sometimes be seen as an individual activity but teamwork can be incredibly valuable at each stage. The downside of this is that it may take longer, but taking time with others to think through and plan long, medium and short term is a good investment. Often working collaboratively helps us to see areas we might have missed alone and can generate many more creative ideas as we spark off one another in discussion and exploration. Using a staged process like the cycle above can help maintain a focus to the process.

Planning to be flexible

One of the challenges of a facilitative approach is that of planning in flexibility. In some ways it is much easier to plan a gathering or session in which every moment is accounted for and scripted. The unforeseen aspects of facilitative processes and the open-endedness of some of the ways we may choose to work calls for flexibility in approach, in timings and in organization. Allow sufficient time for questions, comments and conversation and consider preparing different activities for certain parts of a session, so you have a choice of ways of working depending on the response of the group at the time. Think ahead about timings and build in contingencies in case you need to make things last longer or cut things short. Sometimes I include activities that appear in my plan as 'optional' and that I can put in or take out as time allows. Sweet describes this kind of approach as 'modulating', a skill that he says, 'involves learning to adjust to any situation, identifying the adaptive challenges, and adopting an adaptive temperament, exquisitely calibrated to the moment. It's the ability to spot the unexpected and then adapt to meet its challenges' (2004:183).

Relationship skills

Building and establishing relationships can appear to be something that 'just happens' – some people appear to do it with an ease that has an almost magical quality. In most cases, however, relationships take time, energy, effort and hard work and all facilitators will benefit from developing and honing their skills in establishing and building relationships.

Relationships, as we have already identified, are central to every facilitative process. Marshall (1989) claims that four factors or elements are key in a relationship: love (the most enduring), trust (the most fragile), respect or honour (the most neglected) and understanding (which takes the longest). All these things have to work both ways, so a sense of mutuality is fundamental. This means there is an element of risk within the relationships with any individual or group. To engage in relationship is to open ourselves up and make ourselves vulnerable. In the previous chapter Sally explored important values underpinning good facilitative practice, and it is important that your relationship skills grow out of who you are and are not competences that are 'adopted' in some kind of utilitarian way. They need to be authentic. Simple things like taking the time to welcome people, smiling, using appropriate eye contact and learning people's names are all important and can make a big difference.

Listening skills

Another important aspect of building relationships and facilitating effectively is developing listening skills. Here again avoid adopting a set of practices or techniques that are detached from who you are. Anyone can pretend to listen but genuine listening and attentiveness are skills that need to be developed and that may not come naturally. Some people are drawn to leadership and facilitation roles because they like the sound of their own voice, so be aware of the extent to which you like to dominate conversations, get your own point of view across and have the last word. For some, effective listening, vital to effective facilitation, may involve putting a (perhaps natural) tendency to talk too much on hold in order to be genuinely present to others in the group. The following are suggestions for improving your listening skills in facilitation.

Attentiveness

Tune in to what participants are saying and give undivided attention rather than allowing your mind to wander or beginning to frame your response while someone is talking. Be willing to wait while individuals pull their thoughts together or find appropriate words to express what they want to say. Set aside your own opinions, biases and preoccupations so that you can concentrate on what the person is saying, observing and listening to pick up body language and 'unsaid' things that may be important.

Active listening

Be friendly, gentle, interested and empathetic. Avoid patronizing, criticizing and expressing judgement or disapproval while people are speaking. Encourage people with small verbal or non-verbal cues. If it is helpful, clarify that you have understood by checking what they meant. Sometimes it is helpful to use their own words to do this or reframe simply.

Responding

Be supportive and encouraging in your responses. Value contributions without being gushing. Avoid making assumptions, jumping to conclusions or putting words in someone's mouth. Be willing to repeat contributions if others in the group cannot hear. Use brief comments or open questions to steer discussions. Don't ignore or avoid comments or questions that are difficult or painful but acknowledge and welcome them. And don't be afraid to say when you don't know something.

Holding back

As Sally has highlighted, it is important not to be afraid of silence. It will be important for some members of the group to have thinking time. Avoid interrupting unless you need to intervene for the benefit of the group. Resist any temptation to manipulate conversations and discussions by twisting or changing something someone says to fit your own view or agenda. If you feel yourself becoming anxious or defensive, pause before speaking.

Communication and presentation skills

When considering communication skills in facilitation it is important to think about both written and verbal communication. Facilitators may be called upon to communicate in numerous ways using a range of different skills.

Thinking through beforehand what you want to say, and good preparation, are important if you want to communicate clearly and concisely. Seek to ensure that what you say is understandable, precise and unambiguous. Take into account the context you are in and the background and expectations of those participating. Use non-discriminatory, non-oppressive language and watch your stories and visuals for stereotypes and exclusive language. I know many situations when helpful information or messages have been undermined because the person communicating made wrong cultural assumptions.

Using slang, colloquial language, religious jargon, academic or specialist terminology and 'in' joking or referencing can affect participants' ability to engage with you. Take into account how formal or informal the context is, what is suitable or what is not. Watch unhelpful attitudes and don't make assumptions about what people might be thinking or feeling. Be wise when using humour. Work within your personality. I'm hopeless at telling jokes, mainly because I usually forget the punchline, but I find that funny stories that make a good point are useful because they make a helpful contribution even if no one laughs! Avoid jokes or stories that are sexist, racist or discriminatory in any other way. Feel free to poke fun at yourself up to a point but never use humour as a 'weapon' or to score points against someone in the group. Fortunately, I can never think of witticisms on the spur of the moment but I have seen people leading groups who have used humour to put someone down who was irritating them. They won a laugh but often lost the engagement of the individual concerned and the respect of others in the group.

Think about the volume and speed at which you speak and how you articulate – vary tone, pitch and pace to be congruent with what you are talking about and the material with which you are engaging. Get feedback on your presentation skills, particularly any habits or reflex words or phrases of which you might be unaware. One colleague I worked with over a number of years had a really distracting habit of swinging one of his legs whenever he stood up to speak. It took him a long time to break the habit, but the input and encouragement of others in the team was a key part of his improving his skills.

It is helpful as part of process design to think about any concepts you may need to explain more fully or more simply. Consider how you will make information accessible, perhaps by using visuals, a flip chart, notes, handouts or PowerPoint. For points in the gathering where you want to encourage discussion, conversation, debate or decision-making, think through and prepare some helpful questions in advance.

Asking questions

On the face of it questions can appear quite straightforward, but there is an art to their effective use. Some are likely to be unhelpful. I try to avoid using leading questions (designed to elicit a certain predetermined response), trick questions (designed to catch people out) and multiple questions (four or five rolled into one). Parsloe and Wray (2000) identify some different kinds of question that can be used to good effect by facilitators. Framing and using some of these can be a good way of enhancing your practice.

- *Closed questions* are either questions that can be answered by a simple 'yes' or 'no' or questions where a series of alternatives are given, between which people are asked to choose. These can be useful to check facts or agreement but are not helpful in opening up a discussion.
- *Open questions* don't have a 'yes' or 'no' answer and therefore encourage more thoughtful responses and free discussion. They

encourage people to think through or explore an issue more fully – for example, 'What do you think are the strengths of the proposal?'

- *Awareness-raising questions* encourage people to think about their own response to things that have happened – for example, 'How did you feel when you saw that?'
- *Reflective questions* are used to clarify or confirm what someone is saying – for example, 'You said . . . Can you say a bit more about what you meant by that?' Sometimes we might reframe a contribution and use a clarifying question to check we have understood a contribution properly – for example, 'So are you saying that . . .?'
- *Justifying questions* encourage participants to elaborate more on something or explain something further – for example, 'Can you tell me more about . . .?' or 'Can you develop that a bit further?'
- *Hypothetical questions* are used to apply thinking to a different situation – for example, 'What would that look like if . . .?' or 'How might that work when . . .?'
- *Probing questions* seek to get under the surface of the issues being explored or discussed, either by starting with a broad situation and narrowing down to specifics or by deciding on a focus in advance and digging deeper until you get there.

Notes and prompts

Think about the notes or prompts you will use as you facilitate. Different approaches work for different people and it is important to find one that suits your style. I tend to avoid using a full script as it inhibits flexibility and can come across as quite formal. Some people find typed notes helpful. I tend to use PowerPoint and will usually print myself a copy with three slides to a page and notes at the side. I also often use mind maps – see <www.buzanworld.com> – in certain contexts, particularly in the planning stage.

Co-facilitation skills

Many of us will find ourselves regularly or occasionally required to facilitate alongside others. Co-facilitation has many advantages. It is often helpful to have others to work with in planning and preparing, bringing creative ideas, different perspectives and spotting things we might have missed in our thinking. Another facilitator is likely to bring skills, experience and knowledge into the process that are different from our own, and hopefully these will complement and enrich the whole experience both for us and for those participating. Co-facilitating can assist in our development as we observe someone else's approaches, evaluate together and receive feedback on our own practice.

However, it is important that we think carefully about the process of co-facilitation, not just in terms of what will happen on the day but in ensuring that we are aware beforehand of our expectations, values and assumptions rather than simply taking them for granted.

Several years ago I facilitated some informal training for a church and decided to involve a more experienced colleague to develop my own practice and understanding. He had a background in education and a number of years' experience. We met briefly to discuss his involvement and then clarified some issues in a short telephone conversation. Although I had felt this communication was adequate this proved far from the case. On the day my colleague delivered material that was completely different from what we had agreed and rather than being participative he adopted a lecturing style, presenting huge amounts of information without much interaction or engagement with the group. Although I had briefed him that the group were already experienced in some of the issues on which we were focusing, he addressed them as 'beginners', which unfortunately led to further disengagement and members of the group feeling patronized and bored. On reflection I became aware of how many assumptions I had made about supposed shared values, 'right' and 'appropriate' ways of working, what the word 'participation' meant and what we had agreed in terms of content.

Although I found this experience difficult and painful it has been really formative in the way I would now seek to work with others. Above all, communication and clarity of expectation are crucial when co-facilitating. Ensuring that things that have been agreed are put into writing is helpful, even if this feels a little over-formal. A co-facilitator agreement can provide a framework for discussion, and it will be helpful to explore the following issues when planning to co-facilitate:

- What values do you both have in terms of the purpose of the session and what facilitation is about?
- How would you both describe your styles and what does this look like in practice?
- What will it be helpful to know about each other to help you work well together?
- What will be the balance of power in terms of whether the group will be facilitator-led or group-led?
- What kinds of methodologies and approaches will you use?
- How will you work together? Will you section the time off separately or work as more of a 'double act' throughout?
- Do you have freedom to intervene when the other person is facilitating and vice versa?
- What are your expectations during the session if one of you disagrees with the other? How will this be handled?
- Who will take responsibility for the practical issues that need addressing, such as equipment needed, communication beforehand and afterwards, refreshment, venue?
- How will you evaluate afterwards?

Growing your own style

As we have identified, skills are abilities that can be developed and honed. However, as individuals we will express and manifest them in different ways. It is helpful to work on our strengths, identify and develop those areas where we are weak and seek to stretch ourselves to try new things.

- Seek to embody the message – be congruent.
- Be positive and enthusiastic.
- Own what you are saying.
- Don't try to copy others – by all means learn from them, but find your own style.

For action and reflection

- How would you describe your style as a facilitator?
- Do an inventory of your own skills – what are your strengths and weaknesses as a facilitator? Looking at the areas listed here,

what do you perceive as the areas in which you would most like to grow and develop? Set some very specific goals for your own development.

- If you are not accustomed to co-facilitating, arrange to do this to get the experience. Seek to work with someone who is quite different from you and use the suggestions in this chapter to find effective ways of working together. Reflect on the experience afterwards and identify what you have learnt about yourself and about working with others.
- Think of a context in which you regularly facilitate and frame some questions to use in that context that are different from the kinds you would normally use.

3

Culture setting: creating hospitable spaces

JO WHITEHEAD

> All space is potentially sacred, waiting for the moment of
> encounter in which it mediates God . . . If that is the case, then
> sacred space is bound up with event, with community, and with
> memory.   (Cameron et al., 2005)

In exploring issues around creating appropriate and effective spaces
for facilitation, it is helpful to revisit the notion of hospitality.
I'm sure many of us can think of examples of times when we have
felt welcome and at home because of the hospitality expressed to us.
Equally I'm guessing we can also remember times when we have felt
unwelcome and on edge in situations, meetings, churches and social
encounters.

Hospitality is about more than having a beautiful or comfortable
environment. It is about the way that a place is used, the welcome
given, the attention shown, the sense in which we are made to feel
at ease – or not! Nouwen uses the concept of hospitality to explore
healing and vulnerability in ministry, describing it as

> the virtue which allows us to break through the narrowness of our
> own fears and to open our houses to the stranger . . . Hospitality makes
> anxious disciples into powerful witnesses, makes suspicious owners
> into generous givers, and makes closed-minded sectarians into inter-
> ested recipients of new ideas and insights. (1972:89)

According to Nouwen, hospitality is engendered through concentration – the way we pay attention to others rather than keeping our focus
on our own interests and concerns; and through community – creating a sense of unity that grows out of an awareness of our shared
brokenness and hope.

Whether we feel naturally gifted in the area of hospitality or not, the environment in which gatherings take place can make all the difference between a positive and negative experience, both for facilitators and participants. This not only encompasses issues around physical places but also emotional, relational and spiritual spaces.

Physical space

As facilitators we can underestimate the level of control we have over the physical environments in which we work. Whatever your situation there is much you can do to ensure that the culture you create is conducive to what you are seeking to achieve.

Choosing a venue

The choice of venue is important whenever you are drawing a group of people together for a purpose. Where you choose to meet communicates a great deal about your intention for the gathering. You may be fortunate enough to have access to purpose-built, light, welcoming and comfortable meeting places, but for many in church-based ministry the reality is more likely to be meeting in an older church building, hall, office or in someone's home.

Places carry significant messages and meanings. Some are more neutral than others. Meeting in a home will create a certain atmo-sphere, which could include a sense of warmth, comfort, hospitality and relaxation. However, this is likely to give power, however subtly, to the person whose home is being used. As 'host' they will immediately assume a different relationship to the group. Within some cultures, gathering in homes can feel quite threatening, whereas for others it will be a natural and normal part of what people do every day. Gathering in an office space is likely to carry a more 'work-focused' message and feel. A church hall or building is, in many ways, a more neutral venue but can carry its own messages and expectations.

When choosing a venue, thought should be given to the purpose of the meeting. An informal planning meeting, for example, will have different requirements from a training course or worship meeting. The numbers of those attending is likely to be a key, if not *the* key deciding factor.

Accessibility

Legislation relating to disability discrimination, introduced in 1996 and amended in 2004, requires agencies – including companies, churches and charities – providing a service to take reasonable steps to make their buildings and services accessible to disabled people. In some cases this might mean installing a wheelchair ramp where there is a staircase or ensuring that doorways are wide enough and toilet facilities are accessible to everyone. These issues need bearing in mind when you look at the venues you intend to use for gatherings.

Comfort

When thinking about physical space the issue of comfort – either too much or too little – is important.

- *Seating* of some kind will be used in most if not all gatherings. It is helpful to think about how comfortable the chairs are, especially if people will be sitting for any length of time. The ease with which individuals can get in and out of seats – particularly very low ones – can be an important consideration for older groups or for individuals with back problems. One church I visited met in a primary school – a lovely spacious room but with child-sized seating. The sight of people of all shapes and sizes perched precariously on tiny chairs was an interesting one to behold!
- *Temperature* can be a key factor in people's comfort or discomfort. The heat of a room, or lack of it, will sometimes be beyond our control, but it is helpful to think it through in advance. If a gathering is not a regular one, arrangements may need to be made for heating to be switched on for an extra amount of time. It is also worth checking rooms for draughts and thinking about whether windows should be open or closed. On a very hot day some rooms can be stifling, so you may need to consider bringing in a fan of some kind.
- *Light* can influence an atmosphere significantly. Both extremes can be a problem here. Glaring tube lights can be incredibly offputting, as can a dingy dark environment. Consider whether or not to use curtains or blinds. Think about issues such as sunlight shining on people's faces and how that might affect their ability to focus. Bear in mind the time of day the gathering will be taking place and any implications this may have.

- *Noise* and disturbances can also be an issue. People's focus, concentration and enjoyment can be significantly hindered by disturbances – whether from inside or outside a building. Road works, loud heating systems, a group meeting next door or worship band practice can all be offputting. In a home context it is worth giving thought to the presence of children or pets. However adorable they might be to the parent or owner, they can prove a significant distraction to a well-planned gathering.

Hospitable space

The notion of hospitality is particularly helpful when thinking about the feel of a space. Atmosphere can be created by having music playing in the background as people come in, using good lighting (investing in some cheap uplighters may be valuable in some contexts), using rugs, small tables, visual aids and so on.

Thoughtfulness in terms of refreshments can be helpful to consider too. Having tea, coffee and/or cold drinks available may feel a bit inconvenient, especially if it means bringing everything with you, but it can make a tremendous difference, particularly if people have travelled some distance or have come straight from work. Having some nibbles around – biscuits, small sweets or fruit – need not be expensive but can help create more of an informal and hospitable feel. I find it interesting to see the extent to which people's faces light up when they see a bowl of sweets on a table, for example. Be aware of food issues here, such as allergies or religious issues. Also try to avoid things that are noisy, messy or difficult to eat!

Atmosphere can be created in lots of different ways, and again it is helpful to consider the purpose of the gathering before deciding how to lay out the room. Large spaces can feel inhospitable when occupied by a small group – consider sectioning off a big room by using screens or chairs. If projecting, you can use a projector screen to create an internal 'wall' to demarcate some space. If using a big room for a smaller gathering, consider using different parts of the room for different purposes – for example, having refreshments set up in one part of the room, some big tables with sheets of paper on for a feedback activity and elsewhere some clusters of chairs for the main discussion or activities. The sense of 'things' being around can create interest and intrigue for people as they arrive, and changing between different spaces during the session provides opportunity for movement and stretching, delineates different parts of the session and enables you to be set up in advance rather than trying to change the space around in the course of the session.

Be aware that the more creative you are with the setting the more time you are likely to need to set up and pack away afterwards.

What seating says

Where possible, thought should be given to seating. Sometimes there may be limitations due to the venue (pews are not easily moved, for example), but often a thoughtful, considered approach to the laying out of a room can be beneficial. Again, you need to think here about the purpose of the gathering, the level of communication you envisage, whether you want a focal point or need participants to see a screen or visuals, whether or not tables will be helpful. The following sections consider some approaches to seating.

The lecture (see Figure 4)

Rows inhibit participation. Here the facilitator holds the power. The participants are observers and may communicate with the facilitator but not very easily with each other. This kind of layout gives a very formal feel. It may be useful for a gathering where information is going to be imparted, but it does not encourage participation, co-operation or involvement.

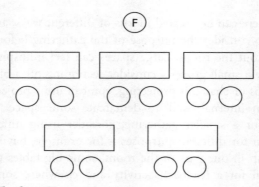

Figure 4 The lecture

The interview (see Figure 5)

The interview (see Figure 5)

Again, this is more formal. I have been in this kind of setting a number of times, and depending on the dynamic of the group it can either feel like a lecture by the facilitator or as if the facilitator is being interviewed by the rest of the group. It feels very 'us and them', the table bringing even more separation between the facilitator and participants.

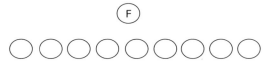

Figure 5 The interview

The conference table (see Figure 6)

This gives a much more collaborative feel. It is still potentially quite formal, with the sense of a job to be done or a task to be accomplished, but there is a sense of equality to the layout, particularly if the facilitator sits in the middle at one side rather than at a far end or the 'head' of the table. This diminishes the power dynamic and encourages participation. The table is helpful if people will need to write, make notes, read information and so on. However, it is not very flexible if you are seeking to break down into smaller groups or move around the room a lot.

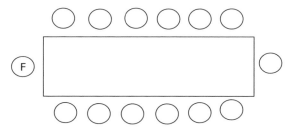

Figure 6 The conference table

The circle (see Figure 7)

This is highly participative and informal and potentially encourages participation and communication all round. It lends itself well to the centre of the circle becoming a focal point – for worship or reflection or with a small table with snacks and/or drinks. Participants who don't know each other can feel quite exposed and vulnerable in this kind of layout, however, as there is nowhere to hide!

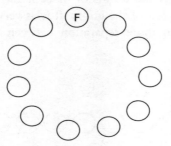

Figure 7 The circle

The horseshoe (see Figure 8)

Again, this is very participative. A little more facilitator-focused but a useful layout if participants need to see a screen or other visuals. It still encourages participation and mutual engagement but again participants can feel a little exposed.

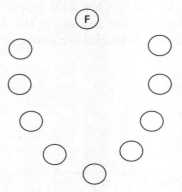

Figure 8 The horseshoe

Clusters (see Figure 9)

This works well with a larger group where you are seeking to encourage conversation within smaller groups and maintain an informal feel. Again, participants can feel a little exposed, but using low coffee tables for each group can help.

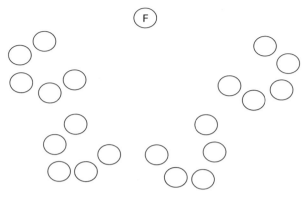

Figure 9 Clusters

Table clusters (see Figure 10)

This is a little more formal but keeps the idea of the clustered group within a group. It can be useful where participants need to talk in groups and make notes, consult handouts or write things down. This approach can be made to feel more relaxed by creating more of a café-style feel with snacks and nibbles on the tables and disposable tablecloths on which people can write, doodle, take notes or give feedback.

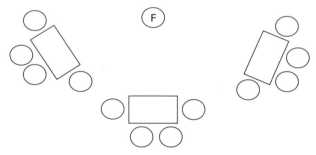

Figure 10 Table clusters

Another aspect to consider in relation to the layout of the room is whether you sit or stand as facilitator. The power dynamics of our posture and position can communicate a great deal. In a larger group I tend to feel more relaxed standing, particularly because I like to wander around, but I will often choose to sit to encourage a sense of equality and participation. If work or discussion in smaller groups is part of your process, you will need to consider whether you join them or not, and if you do, how you do this. Sitting at a table with a group may feel a little intimidating, while standing 'over' a group may feel awkward. I have sometimes found crouching next to the group to offer support, answer a question or clarify an issue to be a good balance between the two.

Emotional climate

Creating a healthy and safe emotional space within the group is an important aspect of the facilitator's role. How you do this will depend on the duration of the gathering, the purpose of the group, whether the group members already know each other and to what extent and any history they might have. Palmer (1983:71) suggests that in addition to hospitality, openness and boundaries are the other essential dimensions to an effective learning space.

Welcoming and introductions

We will look at this area more fully when we consider facilitating beginnings and endings in Chapter 7, but it is helpful to highlight some key points at this stage. Greeting people warmly, introducing yourself and letting participants know how to find key facilities such as toilets and refreshments are all vital in creating an open, hospitable environment. Linked with this is the importance of openness and being clear about what will be happening during the gathering. We need to ensure that who we are and how we are reflects what we are seeking to do. Avoiding put-downs, humour that is out of place, jargon and showing off should help put people at ease.

Contracting and ground rules

It is really important, particularly when working with a new group, to create opportunity to clarify the group's and your expectations – negotiating a group contract or ground rules can be a helpful way of doing this. These provide helpful boundaries in terms of being aware of what is and is not acceptable behaviour and establishing an agreement around this. This agreement will give you an important point of reference if and when you need to intervene at any point to ensure that the emotional space stays safe. Contracting doesn't have to be as formal as it sounds – it can be done quite quickly or more slowly and carefully. The level of complexity will be affected by the purpose of the group and whether it is going to be short, medium or long term.

Areas to discuss and explore may include:

- issues around talking and listening, one person speaking at a time, everyone having the opportunity to contribute;
- attitudes, including respect and the use of non-oppressive language;
- participants having the freedom to question or challenge, but gently and respectfully;
- the importance of individuals owning their opinions and using the 'I' voice to express themselves rather than speaking on behalf of the group;
- confidentiality and what this might mean in the specific context;
- negotiation around drinks, snacks, breaks, taking time out if necessary;
- the freedom to share personal experience at whatever level feels safe.

Once you have established and agreed a group contract it is important to model and re-enforce the agreed ground rules through what you do. Be consistent – if you say it is okay to ask questions or disagree, make sure you don't respond defensively when people do.

In a small group, contracting can be done through a simple discussion at the beginning of the gathering. In other contexts it may be helpful to ask the group to talk to one another in pairs and identify things that will help them participate and feel safe within the group. This will assist quieter members to have their say in the agreed ground rules. I tend then to either take verbal feedback from each pair in turn or use sticky notes to allow people to feed back their suggestions, which can then be discussed, agreed and written up on a piece of flip-chart paper.

I find it helpful then to fix it to a wall. For a regular group you may decide to type it up, print it and laminate it so that it can be used on an ongoing basis. You will find it helpful to revisit the ground rules briefly at the beginning of every session if possible and especially when new members join. Refer to them regularly, particularly but not exclusively when individuals or the group as a whole begin to step over the boundaries.

Modelling permission-giving

Congruence is important in terms of what you communicate, not only by what you say but by what you do. Modelling permission-giving can be helpful in this regard. So, for example, you may say that people have a freedom to help themselves to drinks at any time, but those accustomed to a more formal environment still may not feel free to do this, restrained by their experience of other contexts. If you help yourself to a drink, say, when the group splits into pairs or subgroups for an initial ice-breaker, this models to the group that it is okay to do this.

Spiritual climate

Awareness of our context and purpose is vital in considering what kind of spiritual climate we are seeking to engender. In many if not all ministry contexts, however, it is important to create space for people to recognize, acknowledge and welcome the presence of God in the gathering.

We can do this in a number of ways:

- Extemporary prayer can be useful, but keep it short and avoid using jargon and hype, particularly if the gathering includes people from different denominations or backgrounds.
- Use a simple liturgy, written prayer, reflection or poem.
- Allow a time of silence for quiet reflection on a picture, an object or a particular thought. One of my colleagues uses a singing bowl to good effect to begin and end a period of silence at the start of a gathering.

Try to avoid imposing a spiritual 'style' on the group in a dominant way that might intimidate. The purpose of this kind of activity is to create some space for people to experience and connect with God for themselves. Beware of asking them to pray publicly if you don't know the group and if they don't know each other – and don't ask people to read aloud unless you know they can read confidently.

In groups where people are a mix of Christian and non-Christian or multifaith groups, silence can be a helpful way of encouraging people to take some space for themselves. This can be framed in a way that gives individuals the freedom to include God or not, depending on their background and preference.

For action and reflection

- Reflect on a physical space you regularly use for a group gathering of some kind. Analyse and critique the space using some of the suggestions early in this chapter. What are the strengths and weaknesses of the space in terms of the purpose of the gathering? To what extent does it help or hinder the purpose of the group? What small changes could you make that might improve the way the space works for the group?
- Much of this chapter was written in my local coffee shop. Visit a café or restaurant that you think has a good atmosphere. Spend some time looking around and considering how the atmosphere has been created and whether you could transfer any of the principles to your practice as a facilitator.
- Think about how you present yourself to groups you work with. Consider how you might enable groups to feel more secure.
- Next time you work with a group, experiment with a different seating arrangement and see what happens. Reflect on how the feel of the group changes or not.
- Consider a group that you work with in terms of the sense of emotional and social feel within the group. What kind of culture is there? Is it positive or negative? What acknowledged or unacknowledged ground rules are in place? What could be done to increase further the emotional health of this group?
- Begin to draw together your own collection of resources for mini-reflections to use at the beginnings of sessions to help focus groups spiritually. Consider using sources drawn from Christian traditions other than your own.

4

Group stages, culture and roles

JO WHITEHEAD

> When I am fully alert to whatever or whoever is right in front
> of me; when I am electrically aware of the tremendous gift of
> being alive; when I am able to give myself wholly to the moment
> I am in, then I am in prayer.   (Barbara Brown Taylor)

Self-awareness is vital when we consider the challenges and opportunities of engaging with group dynamics. In ministry contexts we
are likely to find ourselves facilitating many different kinds of groups,
which will vary significantly in the way they are structured, in their
purpose and focus, in the types of people within them, their level
of formality, patterns of meeting, culture, norms and ways-of-being.
Groups don't exist in a vacuum and can be affected and influenced
by an array of contextual and external factors – facilitators are an
integral part of the group, whether or not they perceive themselves
as such.

It is helpful at the outset of this chapter to state that I understand
groups as dynamic, complex and multifaceted. They are organic and
constantly changing as the people within them change, grow and
bring different aspects of themselves into the group context. Groups
are greater than the sum of their individual members, not only in
the possible outcomes but also in terms of the complexity of the
dynamics that will be at work. This has been described as 'group-as-
a-whole' phenomena (Ringer, 2002), and is significant in informing
group facilitation processes.

Group as body

In his letter to the Corinthian church, the apostle Paul, using the
metaphor of the body, illustrates how God's people can work effectively together and suggests some things to help this process:

- valuing each individual as part of the group (1 Corinthians 12.12);
- recognizing that simply not wanting to be part of it doesn't stop someone belonging (12.15);
- acknowledging that each person has a significant role to play (12.17);
- celebrating God's creative design in the way the whole is put together (12.18);
- nurturing mutual interdependence (12.21);
- appreciating that people who appear weaker may be indispensable (12.22);
- understanding distinct ways of working with different individuals (12.23);
- expressing equal concern for each member of the group (12.25);
- realizing that if one suffers all suffer (12.26).

Body ministry at its best will recognize and value each individual, their value and the role they have to play. There will be a sense of mutual giving and receiving, honouring, concern and sensitivity.

Stages of group development

There are various models for understanding the stages that groups go through. Perhaps the most well known is Tuckman's model of forming, storming, norming and performing (1965). Although this model has flaws, it provides a useful framework to consider the way groups develop.

Forming

According to Tuckman, the first stage of group development is the forming stage, when a group comes together and begins to establish its identity. At this point individual group members are likely to be wondering what the group will be like, how they will fit, what the purpose is, whether they really want to be part of it and how others might perceive them. This can create a sense of anxiety and caution – individuals come across as quite wary and watchful. There is likely to be a high level of dependency on the group facilitator during this stage. If some members of the group already know each other, you may need to consider ways their past history can affect forming. To a certain extent forming will take place every time the group gets together, and will certainly happen if someone new joins the group. Even someone arriving late can 'send' a group back into the forming stage.

How to support the forming stage of group development

- Create a welcoming, hospitable, safe environment.
- Clearly communicate the purpose and aims of the group and give as much information as possible about expectations and process.
- Provide opportunities for the group to get to know each other and gel through social interaction and suitable non-threatening activities.
- Establish and agree clear ground rules for working together.
- Recognize the baggage that participants may bring from prior experience and acknowledge how these might inform people's experience and engagement with the group.
- Recognize that how you lead the group is likely to assist in establishing the group norms.

Storming

Once the group has formed, participants begin to feel less wary and start to let down their guard. They begin to assert their individuality more and gain confidence in expressing views and opinions. This is often a time of checking people out and testing the group as a whole to see where the boundaries are, whether they will hold and if it is a safe place to be. Some individuals may over-assert and tend to dominate in this phase. Tensions and difference can lead to disagreements and sometimes power struggles within the group, which can feel quite uncomfortable, perhaps resulting in a sense of 'all or nothing, for or against' (Jaques, 1991:34). Particularly in ministry contexts, group facilitators often find this stage of the group process difficult and may struggle to allow and give space for storming, but this is a key part of the group's development. Wisdom is needed here because if this phase is too long it can be emotionally draining and can actually stop the group from achieving anything.

How to support the storming stage

- Stay calm and don't panic. Try not to be anxious, particularly if you find conflict difficult. Ensure that your own discomfort doesn't inhibit the group from storming.

- Ensure that boundaries are maintained and the group contract is adhered to in order to build a sense of security within the group. Be prepared to challenge language or attitudes where necessary.
- Where possible seek to normalize disagreement and individuality, for example by affirming that it is fine for people to have different views and perspectives.
- While leading firmly, avoid being too directive. Over-directive leadership in this phase can encourage passivity and dependency within the group.
- If a group is trying to storm but struggling, and you sense it is important for them to storm, you may feel it right to encourage the process. This could be done by, for example, staging a debate on an issue and allowing the group to practise disagreeing with one another by discussing from a perspective that is not necessarily their own.

Norming

In this stage emphasis moves from an individual focus to the concerns of the group as a whole. As people relate to one another, group norms really begin to emerge, with a growing sense of collaboration, healthy questioning and listening.

How to support the norming stage

- Encourage positive group norms but be aware that some aspects of the group culture may not be healthy and may need addressing or challenging.
- Be aware of the roles that people are adopting within the group and seek to encourage these to develop in a healthy way.
- As the group develops stronger relationships there can be quite a significant emotional investment into the group from participants. Be prepared to encourage a focus on the task in hand.
- Strong relational connections can also make the group difficult for others to join, and it may be important to help the group consider how they will welcome newcomers.

Performing

If the group is moving positively through the stages, performing is likely to begin during the norming stage, but gradually this should become the habitual way-of-being for the group. As the group moves into a more task-focused way of working, people will become more settled in their roles and patterns of teamwork and collaboration should emerge. At this point group facilitators should be able to adopt a less directive and interventionist role and serve as a resource to the group.

How to support the performing stage

- Be willing to take a back seat and allow the group to take increasing responsibility. See yourself as a resource for the process.
- Stay aware of the need to intervene but only where necessary.
- If new people join the group, seek to find ways of enabling them to flow with the group and feel part of what is going on by allocating a specific role or encouraging another member of the group to support them.

Mourning (or adjourning)

This fifth stage of group development was added to the model later and is a crucial phase in the life of groups that is often neglected. Mallinson (1996:157) suggests five important aspects of closure for the mourning stage of a group: recalling (high points, helpful things, encouragements), confession (brief acknowledgement of areas where hurt might have occurred), thanksgiving (can be done creatively), expressions of hope (for the future personally, for the work, ministry and so on) and farewell.

The importance of ending things well and how this process might be supported is explored fully in Chapter 7.

Group culture and norms

Culture has been described as 'the way we do things round here'. The longer a group exists the more established the culture is likely to become, although even a group that meets together for a relatively short time may develop its own identity and norms, which will influence what happens within the gathering during that time. The group culture will affect communication patterns, what is acceptable and unacceptable behaviour within the group, how the group relates to the facilitator and how the group manages anxiety.

Socialization has been described as 'the process through which an individual learns to be a member of society' (Berger, 1972:62). This occurs first in childhood through 'primary socialization' and then subsequently, though less intensely, throughout life as the individual joins new social groups and engages in processes of 'secondary socialization' (Berger and Luckmann, 1966). Theorists suggest that the willingness to adapt identity to 'fit' the social groups of which we are a part reflects an innate desire to belong and to be able to self-define in a way that makes sense to the individual. To a certain extent, throughout life individuals are constantly adapting and changing their identities to fit and conform to the changing social groups in which they find themselves.

This process of socialization will be at work to a greater or lesser extent in all the groups we facilitate. People may not consciously seek to fit into the group but nevertheless are likely to adapt their behaviour to suit the culture engendered by it. Group norms 'specify, more or less precisely, certain rules for how group members should behave and thus are the basis for mutual expectations among the group members' (Brown, 1988:42). Group norms are important for individuals within the group in terms of helping them have a sense of security and knowing what is expected of them. They also serve to give a sense of identity and cohesion to the group and often enable it to function as a social unit effectively from a task point of view.

Group roles

Closely linked to group culture and norms is the likelihood that people will adopt specific roles within groups. This can happen as a result of people's prior experiences of being part of a group, the expectations of others or their own desires and wishes. Group roles can be adopted both consciously and unconsciously and can be simple or more complex to identify.

Deliberate and 'accidental' role adoption

Sometimes roles are given or ascribed in a formal way. People can be designated particular jobs or roles that then determine how they might behave or act in a group. Roles, whether prescribed or not, can give individuals a sense of security and identity. Like group norms, roles can give a sense of security as they 'imply expectations about one's own and other's behaviour and this means that group life becomes more predictable and hence more orderly' (Brown, 1988:55).

Belbin's team roles

Belbin identified a number of roles that people adopt in teams, a model that is particularly helpful for facilitators working in a more task-focused environment (adapted from Belbin, 1981; 1993).

- *Shapers* are highly motivated leaders with a strong sense of vision, energy and motivation. They are the people in the team who will see ideas pushed through to reality but can become focused on the task at the expense of team relationships.
- *Co-ordinators* are mature, confident leaders with good 'people skills'. They are gifted at seeing where people fit within a team and at encouraging and inspiring them to be involved. They sometimes clash with shapers as they can be more relationship- than task-focused.
- *Plants* are creative, entrepreneurial, intelligent and full of ideas. They tend to operate at some distance from the rest of the team and sometimes find it hard to integrate. They are the most likely to come up with creative ideas but may struggle with implementing and following these through.
- *Resource investigators* are good communicators and negotiators, often having one foot in and one out of the team. They tend to build effective networks of relationships beyond the team and are skilled at identifying available resources and necessary tasks. They can become bored and frustrated by routine and repetition.
- *Team workers* are the backbone of the team. They are sociable, supportive, flexible and adaptable. They are good listeners and committed to supporting relationships within the group. They are often happy not to be involved in decision-making and would rather support others. They may be indecisive at critical times.
- *Implementers* are reliable, disciplined and hard-working. They are well organized and good at seeing what needs to be done and getting on with it. They are more interested in getting the job done than in their own role or success. They are competent and will do what needs to be done, although they may sometimes come across as unimaginative and inflexible.
- *Monitor evaluators* are shrewd and analytical. They are able to think critically and weigh up the advantages and disadvantages of projects and situations. They like to have time to think things over.

They are the people most likely to stop the team from making a mistake but may appear negative and over-critical at times.

- *Completer-finishers* are precise, highly motivated and hard-working. They pay attention to detail and are generally serious-minded and accurate. They are good at keeping to deadlines and keeping the team on track but may be intolerant of those with a more relaxed attitude.

Belbin's model helpfully demonstrates the breadth of skills that are useful to have within a team. You may find this useful when drawing a team together – or when working with existing teams, facilitators will sometimes need to step in to fulfil roles that are not naturally present. Explicit exploration of team roles within a group can be beneficial in addressing conflicts – for example in leadership style – or frustrations, as group members learn to appreciate what others contribute and value differences. You may find it helpful to develop your awareness of the team roles at work within groups you facilitate regularly so that you can draw on specific roles to make strategic contributions at particular times.

Other group roles

In addition to team roles, we might see people adopt a range of other roles, including:

- leader, organizer, instigator, spokesperson;
- stirrer, questioner, provoker, 'devil's advocate';
- clown, joker, entertainer;
- teacher, informer, instructor, advisor;
- summarizer, critic;
- mediator, peacemaker, pacifier;
- gatekeeper, welcomer;
- carer, helper, pastor, encourager;
- rescuer, protector;
- victim, scapegoat.

The majority of these roles are neutral and can work both positively or negatively in terms of the group dynamics. Someone adopting a clown role can bring a helpful sense of fun and light-heartedness to proceedings and can use humour to good effect to release tension, encouraging an open and positive atmosphere. However, a clown who is not self-aware may distract, annoy others, offend through the nature of the humour itself, and by constantly making jokes prevent the group from addressing serious issues. Similarly, a questioner may provoke interesting discussion but taken to extremes this behaviour can feel critical and prevent the group reaching conclusions or making decisions.

Responding to group behaviours

We will explore more complex aspects of working with group dynamics in Chapter 6, but here I suggest ways of responding to some of the most common behaviours within groups.

Silence

There can be many reasons for people being silent in groups, including natural shyness or reticence, the dynamic of the group, fear of being wrong or looking stupid, boredom, lack of interest or simply needing a bit more time to think things through before contributing.

Here are some ways of encouraging quieter people to participate.

- If you know people well, try drawing them in by using their name.
- If you are prone to move on in discussions very quickly, allow a few moments' 'thinking time' before asking for responses from the group.
- Give warning that you are going to ask everyone to say something, then give a few moments for people to consider their contributions before going round members of the group in turn.
- Break people down into pairs or small groups to discuss something before feeding back into the group as a whole.

Dominant members of the group

Dominance can manifest itself in a number of ways. It may be that someone is dominating the conversation or discussion, not allowing others to contribute, or is cutting in across other people. When negotiating ground rules with groups, be explicit about the fact that some people talk more and others are quieter. Encourage the group to make space for one another to speak and contribute. Where necessary during a gathering, gently reaffirm ground rules to encourage dominant participants to listen. Specifically ask for contributions from those who have not yet spoken.

Someone seeking to take over leadership of the group with a more directive, assertive style can be challenging for facilitators. In addressing this kind of behaviour, ensure you don't get into a power struggle with the group member who has assumed a leadership role. Instead, rather than becoming defensive or anxious, stay calm and be secure in your own position within the group – you have nothing to prove. Using a clearly defined process such as discussion in pairs or small groups can provide helpful structure in these kinds of situations.

Clowns, jokers and distractions

With joking, distracting behaviour, maintain clear boundaries, gently using the group contract to challenge particular patterns of behaviour. If an individual's contribution has drawn attention away from an important issue, draw the group back to the point without putting the person down.

Responding assertively

Addressing behaviour issues within the group and assisting groups to work effectively will require assertiveness skills. Assertiveness can be understood as sitting between the extremes of a passive and aggressive response.

Facilitators at the **passive** end of the spectrum tend to avoid any form of conflict or confrontation. They tend to assume that difficulties or struggles within the group are their responsibility and may adopt a victim or martyr role. They may sacrifice the pain of short-term intervention for the sake of peace.

Facilitators at the **aggressive** end of the spectrum will tend to see personal relationships through the lens of power. In difficult situations they are likely to be blunt and competitive, usually assuming that others are in the wrong, and may resort to dominating or bullying verbally to get their own way.

It is clear that both these extremes are unhelpful in facilitation. Passive facilitators rarely address issues effectively, and group members tend either to retreat from aggressive facilitators and 'close down' or adopt an aggressive approach themselves. Equally unhealthy is a **passive-aggressive** approach, where individuals look passive as they avoid direct confrontation but then manipulate, undermine others or recruit support to get their own way.

An **assertive** response is one that accepts self and others and in which facilitators expresses their feelings firmly and calmly. They face up to issues and seek resolution in ways that bring about positive outcomes for all concerned.

If you recognize aspects within your own practice that tend towards the passive, aggressive or passive-aggressive, there are ways of developing more assertive responses.

- Recognize that your opinions, feelings and needs are as important as anyone else's.
- Accept difference – recognize that it is okay for you to be yourself, to question, disagree, express opinions, struggle and make mistakes, and that it is fine for others to do this too.
- Try to become more aware of any underlying issues in your life or history that contribute towards you responding in an unhealthy way – for example, family responses to conflict, fear of what people will think, negative past experiences.
- Accept that you are not going to please everyone all the time.

A helpful tool in developing assertiveness is an 'I statement', which is a way of describing how something is affecting us and what we would like to see change. The first part summarizes the situation briefly, clearly and objectively. The second part expresses how you feel without blaming or accusing. The third part expresses what you would like to see happen. Some examples of using 'I' statements in facilitation would be:

- 'When everyone speaks at once, I can't hear what people are saying and I would like us to speak one at a time so that everyone's contribution is heard and valued.'
- 'When you don't take part in discussions I feel sad because I feel we are missing out on what you have to contribute, and I would really like to hear what you have to say about this issue.'
- 'When you use language like that I feel frustrated because I feel that you are not respecting our group contract – I would like you to keep to the ground rules we have agreed together.'

Personal involvement

In a very real sense, facilitators should be 'in' the group but not 'of' it. It is vital to gain emotional distance and not allow yourself to get so caught up in the group culture and dynamic that you lose perspective. Additionally, seek to avoid being dependent on the group for emotional security or for affirmation.

For action and reflection

- Try to think of at least three different groups of which you have been a part, preferably in very different contexts. How many roles did you adopt? Are these the roles you most commonly adopt in group situations?
- Read 1 Corinthians 12.12–31 and Romans 12.3–8. Spend time reflecting on these two passages and consider what they might have to say to you in terms of your understanding of how groups work. How might the principles here challenge your own practice in facilitating groups?
- Reflect on where you sit personally on the passive–assertive– aggressive spectrum. How do you tend to respond in difficult situations?
- Think of a challenging interpersonal situation you are facing or have faced. Construct one or two 'I' statements that you could use in this situation.

5

Creative approaches to facilitation

JO WHITEHEAD

> Life is creative. It plays itself into existence, seeking out new
> relationships, new capacities, new traits. Life is an experiment
> to discover what's possible. As it tinkers with discovery, it
> creates more and more possibilities. With so much freedom
> for discovery, how can life be anything but playful?
>
> (Margaret Wheatley and Myron Kellner-Rogers, 1996:9)

The fingerprints of an infinitely creative God are scattered across history. From the speaking of the first creative word in the opening chapter of Genesis, through the subsequent unfolding of God's purposes, we see an unbelievable display of imagination, a celebration of diversity, striking examples of humour and incredible attention to detail. In the highs and lows of God's relationship with humanity we witness outrageous variety in the way the Creator communicates, using rainbows, burning bushes, donkeys, angels, dreams and weather to meet each person where they are. God's own personality and splendour are reflected in creation to such an extent that 'the heavens declare the glory of God' and 'They have no speech, they use no words; no sound is heard from them' (Psalm 19.1, 3). We see this creativity reflected too in the life and ministry of Jesus, who exemplifies creative approaches to communication, using story, object lessons, everyday life, parables, brain-teasers, imagery, practical demonstration, miracles, modelling and participation to engage with believer and sceptic alike.

The evidence that those who are made in the image and likeness of this creative God mirror his creativity can be seen throughout human history. The use of the *mezuzah* in Jewish culture, which encouraged members of the household on leaving and entering the home to reflect on their allegiance to God, is just one example of the rich way God's people were encouraged to learn and remember their heritage through the use of symbol and imagery (Sweet, 2000a:17). Within the Church, people have striven to express worship through creative expression – the fashioning of architecture designed to reflect the glory and majesty of God, the use of music, art and liturgy all illustrate this. The medieval musical practice of Gregorian chants, iconography within the Orthodox tradition and the Celtic use of poetry and song are examples of ways in which God's people have embraced creative approaches to worship and learning.

The post-Reformation focus on word-based approaches to faith and learning appears to have robbed the Church of some of the creativity prevalent in biblical times and earlier expressions of Christianity (Fleming Drane, 2002:124). The modern western world crystallized this, with its emphasis on intellect, reason and order. Mystery, images, metaphors and story were sidelined by many and considered illogical and mystical (Sweet, 2000b:86). In today's western culture, where sign, symbol and image dominate, it is perhaps unsurprising that sectors of the Church are beginning to embrace these once again. This, I believe, gives us an opportunity to rediscover strands of our Christian heritage and essential aspects of what it means to be made in the likeness of a creative God. And the exploration can manifest itself in the way we facilitate in a range of contexts.

One reason why people are reluctant to use creative approaches in facilitation is that they don't perceive themselves to be particularly 'arty'. The assumption that creativity is related mainly or solely to the arts is pervasive but, I believe, wrong. I subscribe to a 'democratic' understanding of creativity (NACCCE, 1999:28) – in other words, I believe we are all made in the image of the Creator and have the potential to think and act creatively. How that creativity is expressed will differ from person to person and in different situations, but that sense of diversity is in itself a mark of God's inventiveness.

It is important to emphasize that when I speak about using creative approaches I'm not referring to creative activities designed as ice-breakers or ways in, before we get to the 'real' stuff we are hoping to facilitate. The use of creativity as an attention-grabber before the real business begins has some merit, but I believe that creative approaches are invaluable tools *within* facilitation processes.

Benefits of creative approaches

Although some people see creative activities as being relevant only to certain types of people or age groups, depending how you use them they can be made relevant to all. In fact creative approaches, when used effectively, can break down barriers of age, maturity, class, culture and ability. At their best they will be engaging and fun. Although not everything you do will appeal to everyone, by using different approaches you can bring a sense of vitality and variety into gatherings and engage with varied preferred learning styles.

Many creative approaches involve moving around, which can be very helpful in terms of energizing a gathering, giving variety and helping to engage those who prefer to be active in the way they work and learn. Most are also participative and interactive in some way.

Creative approaches can engage with the whole person rather than simply being focused on the cognitive or thinking domain. Often we will be touching people's feelings, history, opinions and values and engaging with different senses. This multisensory approach is helpful in terms of focus, attention and making what we do engaging and memorable.

When working creatively it is important to recognize that some people might find these kinds of approaches threatening and may be anxious or nervous about doing something creative. If you're working with a group that is used to predominantly word-based approaches, build bridges gradually towards a more creative approach – for example, by using more visuals and some of the simpler participative activities outlined here.

Incorporating visuals

Incorporating visuals into your practice can be a helpful first step towards a more creative approach. Be aware of any people in the group who may be visually impaired and need visuals explaining or require alternative ways of accessing the material.

Using PowerPoint

PowerPoint or other similar software can provide visual interest and cues to some presentations and gatherings. You will need to consider first of all if it is going to be a help or a distraction and if the room and seating arrangement you are using is conducive to this kind of presentation. If you decide to use PowerPoint, here are some key things to bear in mind.

- Plan the presentation – don't have too many slides, and try and keep a theme and flow throughout in terms of the colours, types of pictures and fonts you use.
- Consider the length of time you will display each slide (this is linked to how many you decide to show). Avoid flicking through them quickly – leave enough time for people to read the slides and/or take in any visuals and perhaps note some things down.
- Choose colours carefully, ensuring you have enough contrast between the words and background. If you use pictures as backgrounds, check you can still read any words. Be aware that how the presentation looks on a computer screen will differ from how it will look when projected. Check that your font size is big enough – I usually use a minimum of 28 point.
- Be sparing in terms of content. Use the words on screen for emphasizing key points, summarizing or highlighting an interesting quotation or fact. Don't use too many facts and figures and don't put a 'script' on the screen that you then read.
- Use a combination of visual images along with words. Ensure you use high quality images and either check permissions or use your own photos.
- Animations can be useful and can create interest, but keep them simple. Complex and over-clever animations can be distracting and annoying.
- Make sure you are familiar with the technology, that you know how it works and have time to set it up beforehand.
- Think about where you will sit or stand, what you will project on to and the relationship between the two. You will either need to be somewhere where you can reach the computer or will need a remote mouse or clicker to move the slides on from a distance.

Using flip charts

Flip charts have historically been part of the facilitator's toolkit, but it is helpful to consider how they can be used to their full potential. Some people go to a great deal of trouble to prepare flip-chart pages in advance of a session. Others simply use them as a way of highlighting key points, illustrating diagrams or charts or recording group feedback. I find them useful for group mind-mapping and gathering post-its. I will also often use flip-chart paper to give to small groups or pairs to map or note their feedback, thoughts or impressions.

Simple principles around using a flip chart include considering where you place it in the room – this should be taken into consideration when planning seating and room layout. Where you stand in relation to the flip chart is also important. Similar principles apply as to PowerPoint with regard to visibility, the amount of information on a page and the balance between images and words. In addition to this you will need to think about having the right pens, sufficient paper, seeking to write legibly and ensuring you know how to spell key words. Use of colour, bullet points, underlining and – depending on your drawing ability – pictures will enhance the visual impact.

If you use flip charts regularly, consider developing the way you use them by using more creative graphics, different colours or fonts and experimenting with different page layouts, symbols, bullet points and other visual cues. Where space is more restricted or where you are not able to transport a flip chart, consider using a more flexible approach such as magic whiteboard, which is sold on a roll, can be cut to size and clings to a wall or board. This uses whiteboard pens and can be employed in much the same way as a flip chart – <www.magicwhiteboard.co.uk>.

Practical suggestions

This section gives suggestions for creative activities to use in facilitation. Although they are grouped under specific headings, I have used most of them for a range of purposes and in differing settings. You will find other suggestions for creative approaches throughout Chapters 7 to 12, as we explore different specific contexts. You may well already use some or all of these, but if so I hope their inclusion here will spark other thoughts and ideas. It is important to play to our own creative strengths, interests, gifts or skills, but also valuable to try new things, stretch ourselves and move out of our comfort zones.

Some creative approaches to discussion

Fishbowl

A fishbowl is a way of working with a group whereby a number of chairs are put in a larger circle and part of the group watches another part undertake an activity, discussion or role-play. In a discussion a fishbowl may be set up so that those observing can tap someone on the shoulder and take their turn.

This approach can work well with a large group as a way of encouraging participation. With a group that doesn't know one another well, ensure a safe space by putting good boundaries in place so people don't feel exposed or embarrassed.

Mind map

Map a discussion visually on a flip chart, dry wipe board, large sheet of paper or strip of wallpaper. This can be done on the wall or floor, whichever is best. Write up key words and, if you are able, illustrate these with simple pictures. If you don't feel confident doing this, see if there is someone in the group who would be able to do this well and would enjoy it. Care is needed here to ensure that the visual accurately represents the flow of the discussion rather than just the points with which you personally agreed.

Finish the sentences

Give participants a series of sentences to finish that relate to the subject at hand but are open enough to spark ideas and discussion.

Put your money where your mouth is

This can be a helpful way of increasing participation when seeking to decide on a number of different options or ways forward. Write the different options on sheets of A4 paper and put around the room. Give each person an identical amount of Monopoly money or toy coins and ask them to 'invest' it where they are most committed – they can spread it around or put it all in one place. This gives everyone a say and avoids dominant members swamping the discussion. Open up for discussion and exploration afterwards. This activity can also be used as a way of making a decision when an impasse has been reached.

Collage

Rather than simply discussing or talking about a topic, provide a range of magazines or newspapers and ask people to cut out words and images that remind them of the situation being discussed or explored and that raise relevant issues or questions. Create individual or group collages to reflect people's thoughts, feelings and opinions. This kind of approach can provide more creative insights into situations.

Lists and priorities

Using pieces of paper, post-its or individual dry wipe boards, ask participants to list thoughts and ideas on a subject or issue – perhaps everything they can think of or their top ten. Then encourage them to highlight the top three as a way of focusing on what their most important issues are.

Some creative ideas for getting feedback

Clothes line

Ask people to write different thoughts, ideas or contributions on blank postcards or small pieces of paper then peg up on a clothes line. Gather round the clothes line to look at the contributions and use the pegs to rearrange or group ideas to identify connections or agree priorities.

Post-it notes

Give post-it notes to small groups or pairs and encourage them to write down individual contributions, comments, questions or thoughts. As the group time draws to a close, rather than taking verbal feedback ask each group to come up and stick their post-its on a flip chart or wall. As you draw things together and summarize the feedback, you can group the post-its, create patterns and identify common themes or questions that are emerging. This is an effective way of increasing contributions or giving people the opportunity to ask questions they may be reluctant to pose in front of the whole group.

Bubbles

Use speech or thought bubbles as a way of getting people to feed things back that they think or would want to say on an issue. These can be bought online or created using 'insert shapes' in a Word document.

Be a brick

Buy some wallpaper with a brick wall design on (or paint your own!). Roll this out or stick it on a wall or table. Ask people to write their feedback on a brick. Alternatively, buy hexagonal post-its or 'hexies' – <available from www.teamtalk.co.uk> – and create a honeycomb effect. This approach is helpful in identifying a sense of working together and collaboration in thinking. Lego or Duplo bricks or even Jenga can be used in a similar way for a more three-dimensional approach. Use OHP pens for a one-off or ask people to write on sticky labels so that the bricks can be reused on another occasion.

Posters

Ask groups to feed back by creating a simple poster that summarizes the ideas, thoughts or discussion that have taken place in the group through simple images, colour, words and a key strapline.

Twenty words

Ask people to pick out the most important and significant aspects of their conversation or discussion and summarize these in 20 words. This is a good way of limiting the contributions of more vocal members of the group.

Getting into the Bible

Poems or songs

Find a poem or song that connects with the story, character or theme you are planning to explore. Print the words out so that people can look at them and reflect on them. Play the song or read the poem, perhaps more than once. Give space for people to express their thoughts, feelings and responses to the poem or song and then use this as a way into the Bible passage or story.

Lectio divina

Lectio divina is a five-stage process rooted in the monastic tradition and focused around listening to God. It is not seen so much as a method or technique but as a means of developing relationship with God. Although it is often used for individual reading and reflection, it can be effectively used within a group setting. The five stages of the process are listed here.

1 *Silencio* (be silent) – give space for people to still themselves before God.
2 *Lectio* (read) – read a short passage of Scripture aloud, slowly and carefully, allowing space and time for the words to sink in.
3 *Meditatio* (meditate) – read the passage again, very slowly, perhaps once or twice. Encourage those listening to focus on words and phrases that stand out to them. Stay with these, reflecting on them and allowing thoughts, feelings or images to arise from them.
4 *Oratio* (pray) – encourage people to bring these thoughts, feelings or images to God in silent prayer, recognizing God's love and acceptance.
5 *Contemplatio* (contemplate) – encourage people to take time to rest in God's presence and simply receive from God.

At the end of the process give space for people to share their thoughts and reflections if appropriate and/or to write down anything that has particularly struck them during the time.

Hot seating

This seeks to get behind the words on the page of the Bible. It is helpful if you are confident up-front or if you have someone in the group – or someone you can invite in – who enjoys drama and has a good biblical understanding. Hot seating is basically a form of interview where one person role-plays a particular character from the Bible and others in the group can ask questions. It works best if the group has had the opportunity to hear the story and reflect on it first. Then sit the character in the centre of the room and invite people to ask questions relating to their experience in the story concerned. The person should stay in character throughout.

Case studies or problem pages

To help people explore different themes or questions within a Bible story, prepare short case studies or write a couple of problem-page letters that touch on some of the issues raised. Give people time in pairs to respond to the case study or write a letter in reply to the problem.

Timeline

To explore a Bible story or the life of a particular Bible character, map out the story or life on a long piece of wallpaper. Start with a line highlighting key events and then go back to different key points and add more details through asking questions like those given here.

- How might this person have been feeling at this time?
- What questions might they have had?
- Where was God at work here?

Encourage the group to write their thoughts and responses in different coloured pen and use as a basis for further discussion.

Creative ideas for exploring or expressing feelings

Care is needed when working with feelings and emotions in a group context, but sometimes creative approaches can be very effective in helping people engage with their own responses to a situation and finding ways to express these within the group. The issue of safe space becomes particularly important here, and people should be encouraged to share at whatever level they feel able. These approaches may be particularly useful to begin sessions, in times of transition, for evaluation, endings or when the group is working through difficulties or conflict.

Feelings faces

Use a sheet of paper with simple line drawings of various faces expressing different emotions. Encourage people to identify which face or faces they relate to most and why. Alternatively, print off copies of emoticons.

Mr Men and Little Miss

The Mr Men and Little Miss books provide a range of characters that can helpfully be used to encourage people to express how they feel at a particular time, about a specific issue or more generally. If you have the books you could bring a set in. Alternatively, use pictures of the characters as a way into discussion and exploration.

Words and phrases

Collect a range of words and phrases from newspapers and magazines in different colours and fonts. Back these individually on plain paper and laminate them to use with groups. Scatter them across a table or floor and ask participants to choose one or more that summarize how they feel.

In the news!

A similar approach can be taken with news headlines, although these may need to be used a bit more metaphorically!

Paint your mood

Provide paints and paper and encourage the group to paint their feelings or responses by using colours, shapes or patterns that express something of how they are feeling. Emphasize that the task is not about artistic ability but rather about self-expression!

For action and reflection

- In what ways are you creative? Think broadly, setting aside some of the more common 'artistic' understandings of the word.
- What advantages and disadvantages can you identify in using creative approaches to facilitation?
- What might inhibit you from using creative approaches?
- Choose one of the creative suggestions in this chapter that is different from how you normally work and use it as part of your own devotional or reflective time.
- Identify a friend, colleague or someone in your church or organization you see as very creative. Spend some time talking with that person about how he or she works creatively and uses that creativity.
- Consider pulling together a small toolkit of creative materials to use with groups.

6

Conflict, criticism and effective interventions

JO WHITEHEAD

This is a spirituality that facilitates problem-solving and agreement. The spiritual nature of this work does not replace appropriate techniques and tools, well-honed skills and collaborative processes. Rather it is the fertile soil out of which they grow. It is the essence that gives them meaning and renders them powerful.   (Carolyn Schrock-Shenk)

Intervening in groups to address conflict, confrontation, unhelpful behaviour or personal criticism is perhaps one of the most demanding aspects of facilitation. The complex, multifaceted nature of group dynamics and interpersonal relationships means that responding to challenging situations in groups can be emotionally draining, and it requires self-awareness, emotional intelligence, spiritual maturity, wisdom and dependence on the Holy Spirit.

Schrock-Shenk (1997:24) emphasizes the importance of focusing on 'being' rather than 'doing' in relation to working with conflicting groups. She suggests that a key aspect of this kind of work is relinquishing our own need to be in control and to 'fix' others and situations, nurturing instead an awareness that in our weakness, God's grace will be manifest (2 Corinthians 12.9). While dependence on God provides the 'fertile soil' in which we work, key skills, tools and approaches will assist us in responding effectively in a range of challenging group situations.

Managing emotions and feelings

Managing your own emotions and those that emerge within the group does not mean negating or quashing emotions but rather acknowledging them as inevitable and valuable, and learning to respond appropriately.

Your own feelings

Sometimes unexpected feelings will emerge relating to what is happening while you are facilitating. A comment or a clash with someone in the group may provoke an emotional response. Other reactions may relate to your history, previous experience, vulnerabilities, insecurities or current situations in your life. Growing in self-awareness involves becoming increasingly conscious of behaviour, words and situations that trigger an emotional response in us.

Anxiety

One of the most common emotional responses facilitators experience is that of anxiety, either coming from their own issues or concerns or arising from within the group. Feelings of anxiety manifest similarly to other experiences of stress – we may feel tension in our bodies, embarrassment and even sensations of panic or going blank. In such situations, pause and breathe, then respond out of your values rather than your feelings. Seek to value and accept the person or people concerned, while maintaining the boundaries of the group. Thompson et al. (1998:101) suggest a five-stage process of recognizing the triggers, acknowledging the issues, understanding the cause of the reaction, addressing it alone or with others and then planning a response in case the situation arises again.

Anger

Anger and irritation can easily spill over in a facilitation context. As well as sudden anger, beware of frustration of the ongoing variety, which is simply internalized anger. Deal with irritations as they arise rather than allowing them to build up. If you find yourself getting angry, avoid the temptation to use a well-constructed put-down or crushing humour, especially if you are adept at sharp repartee.

Other emotional responses

A whole range of other emotional responses can arise during facilitation processes. Embarrassment, self-consciousness, nervousness – among others – can all be offputting and even paralysing if they grip us unexpectedly. As well as emotional responses within the group itself, other things happening in your life may affect your emotional state or responses. Personal struggles, stress or tiredness can all manifest themselves unhelpfully. It is important to take a step back and reflect on what has happened, considering what the incident reveals about your own emotional health and, if particular issues or patterns emerge, perhaps working these through with a friend, colleague, supervisor or counsellor. When facilitating it is helpful to practise containment, putting your own feelings on hold – I sometimes visualize myself putting them on a shelf – and concentrating on being present for the group. Sally addressed the issue of self-disclosure in Chapter 1, and you may decide to be open with the group about how you are feeling. If so, it is important not to use the group to meet your own emotional needs by playing the victim and/or encouraging it to rescue or look after you.

Strong emotions in groups

As well as considering your own emotional needs and health you will also need to be prepared to respond to strong feelings that emerge within the group. When strong emotions are present they will not always be expressed in the best or most helpful way. Sometimes your role will be to maintain a safe environment through boundary management. Acknowledging the emotional response, rather than ignoring it, and treating it as 'normal' will go a long way to managing any anxiety that may arise in the group. You may need to give the group some time out, allow some space for reflection or engage in problem-solving. There may also be a pastoral need to pick up on specific issues afterwards or signpost individuals to further sources of help and support.

Emotional intelligence

Daniel Goleman (1996) identifies a range of personal competences that contribute towards emotional intelligence. These will be helpful in your work with groups and in considering your own emotional development. They include:

- self-awareness, including understanding how you feel and why;
- self-mastery, including having control over your feelings and emotions;
- emotional literacy, including understanding the feelings of others;

- empathy, including having compassion for the feelings of others;
- social arts, including connecting with others through developing rapport and relationship.

In seeking to work in emotionally intelligent ways, the following principles are also helpful:

- Seek first to understand and then to be understood (Covey, 1989:237). This involves taking time to listen attentively and actively rather than trying to communicate your own opinions immediately. Ensuring you have genuinely understood where another person is coming from can send a powerful message and will assist you in responding well rather than making assumptions.
- Choose to respond rather than react. This involves pausing, remembering your values, taking a moment to actively seek God's wisdom and choosing to respond with grace, love, truth and integrity. An attitude of humility does not mean assuming you are wrong and others are right but will help you approach situations willing to listen and learn.
- Care for yourself emotionally and spiritually through doing life-giving activities, having effective support and/or supervision and nurturing yourself spiritually. Amid difficult situations this might include practising mindfulness to get back in balance (Runde and Flanagan, 2008) or finding other effective ways of calming and centring yourself.

Appropriate interventions

Between the two extremes of over-reacting and doing nothing it is important to find effective ways of responding to issues, problems and difficulties that arise in groups. There are times when it is important to intervene. For example, when oppressive or discriminatory things are said within the group you cannot simply let them stand or you risk colluding with what has been said. Intervening here can feel difficult as people generally don't intentionally put others down or discriminate against them, and challenging in ways that might embarrass, humiliate or shame someone will simply augment the problem.

Thompson (1998:217; 2006) suggests 'elegant challenging' as a helpful way forward. This involves raising the issue, but in a helpful rather than aggressive or accusatory way. Elegant challenging focuses on the behaviour rather than the person, avoids personal attack and broaches the subject sensitively, seeking to be supportive:

- be tactful and constructive – don't engage in personal attack;
- avoid cornering people;
- allow people to save face;
- choose the time and place carefully;
- don't be punitive;
- undertake any challenge compassionately;
- approach the issues without being confrontational.

Responding to criticism

Buckingham describes criticism as 'one of God's finest shaping tools' (1978:16). However true this may be, being criticized, particularly publicly, can be difficult and painful. Learning to respond healthily to criticism – both on the spot and later – is an important skill.

Your natural reaction to criticism is likely to reflect your tendency towards either a passive or aggressive response. Walton (2012) highlights the danger of responding childishly to criticism, whether our childish reaction is visible or not, and emphasizes the importance of addressing any unresolved childhood wounds. Our response is likely to depend in part on whether the criticism is justified and how it is communicated. It is important to recognize our own internal reactions, while seeking to exercise self-control in what we say and do. Some helpful things to consider listed here:

- Resist the urge to react aggressively or defensively. Receiving the criticism graciously and saying you will consider it often disarms the critic and gives you space to think.
- However unhelpfully the criticism is framed, ask God to reveal any grain of truth within it from which you can learn.
- Where the criticism is unjustified, seek to put it to the side. Consider carefully if a response is needed and, if so, how this should be framed. Communicate any response calmly and assertively, seeking to avoid defensiveness.
- If you find criticism difficult, avoid lapsing into self-blame, rehearsing or obsessing. If you find yourself dwelling on the criticism, seek support and prayer from others, without recruiting support against the critic.

We all make mistakes, and if you make one in a facilitation context, don't try to cover it up and gloss over it. If you respond quickly to address the situation through apologizing or seeking to repair any harm caused, you demonstrate integrity and model effective responses to others in the group.

Responding to conflict

Conflict has been defined as 'any situation in which interdependent people have apparently incompatible goals, interests, principles, or feelings' (Runde and Flanagan, 2008:22). Although we may find conflict difficult because of our own history, upbringing and/or experience, it is a normal aspect of group life. Biblically, conflict is certainly part of the texture of relationships, and many if not all of the great men and women of God seem to struggle with interpersonal issues at times – within families (Jacob in Genesis 27, Joseph in Genesis 37), around leadership (Miriam and Aaron in Numbers 12, Saul in 1 Samuel 19), in churches (1 Corinthians 1) and mission (the dispute between Paul and Barnabas in Acts 15).

According to Runde and Flanagan (2008), common sources of conflict in groups include:

- differences in personality, preferences, styles, values and principles, culture, knowledge and experience, interests and needs;
- feelings of incompatibility;
- unmet expectations;
- factors such as time pressures and heightened emotion.

Some tools and strategies

Understanding mental models

Mental models, otherwise known as 'internal working models' (Ringer, 2002:35), are 'deeply held internal images of how the world works, images that limit us to familiar ways of thinking and acting' (Senge, 2006:163). We all carry these mental models around with us, and they form a foundation to our expectations of how people will see and respond to us. They can contribute to conflict as we become blinded by our own preconceived ideas about people and situations rather than being open to other possibilities about what might be going on.

In a conflict situation we can help people reassess their mental models by encouraging them to take a step back and look more reflectively or objectively at what is happening. This might involve reframing a situation, considering how it might look from different perspectives or using a mapping tool (see page 77).

Talking and listening

Kahane (2004:56) suggests that politeness is one of the key barriers to addressing and solving tough problems. He sees politeness as a 'way of not talking' and suggests that people don't say what they really think or feel because of the fear that relationships will be damaged. Effectively using communication skills, assertiveness skills and encouraging individuals to 'own' what they say through using the 'I' voice will be helpful here.

Transactional Analysis (TA)

TA is a well-known and widely used theoretical approach to human relationships. It explores the ways people relate to each other using three ego-states: parent, adult and child. Thompson (2006) highlights the usefulness of this model in conflict situations. Some of these ego-states can be used habitually by individuals and within groups, leading to unhealthy 'transactions'.

- *Parent–Child* – if you adopt a parental, authoritarian attitude towards someone, you put that person under pressure to adopt a 'childlike' role in response. This works the other way round too. When participants behave in childish ways, you may find yourself adopting a parental tone in response.
- *Parent–Parent* – if you adopt a parental attitude towards someone in the group and that person resists, he or she may try to parent you in return. This can become a destructive power play and lapse into a child–child interaction.
- *Child–Child* – in this kind of interaction neither party takes responsibility. This can result in a lighthearted fun approach but can also easily become destructive moaning and result in a high-dependency and blame culture.
- *Parent–Adult* – this tends to happen when one person tries to parent another but that person resists it by staying 'in adult'. This is a more helpful way to respond.

75

- *Adult–Adult* – ideally this is the kind of helpful interaction you should be aiming for. Although one person may still have authority in the situation, he or she treats the other with respect and as an adult.

TA can help us to recognize our own patterns of reacting and responding in difficult situations and to resist going into child or parent inappropriately. We can also support others in the group to stay in an adult ego-state by speaking to them as adults and refusing to parent them. At times it may be right to challenge patterns of unhelpful childish or parental response, but it should be done sensitively and appropriately.

Mediation

Mediation is a facilitated process and may be used formally or informally when a relationship has broken down or individuals or groups are in conflict. As with other facilitative processes, a safe, boundaried environment, good listening skills and a supportive framework are key to mediation. Mediators seek to assist people in understanding and communicating with one another so that disagreements can be worked through and resolved. Mediators will generally not have authority in a situation but seek to remain impartial. In many ministry settings the different textures of power and authority will need to be acknowledged as we may end up mediating in our own contexts as well as in contexts where we have no responsibility or formal role. Mediation processes usually involve (Macbeth and Fine, 1995:152):

- *opening* – welcome, setting boundaries and ground rules;
- *listening to what happened* – each party summarizes the situation;
- *stating what each person wants* – mediator asks questions to clarify and then summarizes;
- *finding solutions* – establishing what each party is willing to do and finding solutions that are realistic, specific and balanced;
- *agreeing* – reviewing and confirming points of agreement;
- *closing statement* – affirmation, conclusion, thanks.

Negotiation

Negotiation involves similar strategies to mediation but is focused more around discussing each party's needs, demands and interests and agreeing which aspects should be incorporated into a solution. The success of negotiation is dependent on a willingness of both parties to compromise rather than stay entrenched in established positions. The aim in negotiation is to seek to find a win-win outcome that will satisfy both parties. Macbeth and Fine (1995:144) outline possible stages in a negotiation process:

- *preparation* – clarifying what is wanted;
- *discussion* – each side stating their position;
- *proposing* – movement begins as suggestions are made ('What if . . . , then perhaps');
- *bargaining* – parties begin to move towards each other through 'give and take';
- *agreeing* – parties come to an agreement (it may be helpful for this to be put in writing).

Perspective taking

Perspective taking (Runde and Flanagan, 2008) aims to see the conflict from a different point of view and seeks to grow a sense of understanding, empathy and appreciation for all those involved. One way of gaining perspective is to map a situation. A number of models can be helpful.

- *mind-mapping* (Buzan, 2010) uses key words and images to map out situations and establish connections between them. It can also assist in thinking creatively about solutions.
- *eco-maps* (Thompson, 2006) map out relationships across groups of people. To create an eco-map, put the person involved at the centre of a piece of paper and draw the connections and/or relationships as a set of lines, using different colours or types of line – dotted, dashed, jagged, wavy – to highlight relationships that are positive or negative, conflicted, variable and so on. You can add pictures, notes, symbols or metaphors to suit.

When facilitating conflict with a well-established, mature group, consider asking people to map out how they see the group or how the group feels to them, and use this as a base for exploration. This is quite a vulnerable process, however, and good boundaries need to be in place.

Unconscious processes in groups

Identifying and understanding unconscious processes in groups is not an exact science. Indeed, it has been suggested that interpretations of group behaviour are probably 25 per cent right 25 per cent of the time (Jaques, 1991:4). Objective analysis may help facilitators work out what is happening in groups, but qualities such as intuition and awareness also play a significant role. Identifying unconscious processes is as much about learning to understand the feel of the group as about clinical observation.

Basic assumptions

The basic assumption of a group (Bion, 1961) is an unconscious, group-level defence mechanism that provides a means of avoiding the painful processes of learning and growing together and seeks to guarantee the survival of the group. To identify the basic assumptions of groups, facilitators, as participant-observers, need to develop strategies that allow them consciously to opt out of the group as a whole in order to observe less subjectively. Simultaneously, intuitive skills can be used to tap into what is happening (Ringer, 2002:142).

Dependence

Basic assumption dependence normally manifests itself in the group depending on an individual – often the facilitator – to give security and meet their needs (Bion, 1961). Dependent groups can feel exhausting and draining to work with. They may be:

- excessively admiring of the facilitator;
- reluctant to contribute, participate or take responsibility;
- more positive about facilitator-led than participative processes;
- competitive in gaining the facilitator's attention;
- unwilling to function in the facilitator's absence;
- fearful and insecure when demands are made.

Factors including hierarchical leadership models, clergy–laity divide, legalistic or fundamentalist viewpoints and a strong reliance on history can contribute to dependence within Christian groups, leading to a kind of 'institutional dependence' that can be difficult to address.

Fight/flight

With a fight/flight mentality it is as if the group has come together either to fight an enemy or run away from it (Bion, 1961). A tendency to **fight** might be identified by the apprehension of an external 'enemy' (possibly the facilitator, the organization or even the task); feelings of hostility, anger or resentment; backbiting or gossiping; and unproductive arguments not focused on specific or relevant issues. It is important to differentiate this from normal processes of storming within groups. With fight mentality, conflict is unproductive and serves no positive or visible purpose.

Groups use **flight** to avoid anxiety, normally through silence, humour, extended discussion on irrelevant or pedantic issues or an inability to focus on the task. In one team I led, the preferred mode of flight was humour, and in times of anxiety the group consistently looked to one individual to play the clown and rescue them in this way.

Pairing

Basic assumption pairing occurs when the group focuses its attention on a twosome in the group. It is as if this pair is expected to produce something messianic that will guarantee the group's 'salvation' (Bion, 1961:151). This might manifest itself in two individuals engaging in prolonged discussion or debate and consistently becoming the focus of attention. Pairing is the most difficult basic assumption to recognize.

Effective responses

We have already noted the potential difficulties for facilitators in maintaining sufficient detachment to identify unconscious processes. To make any effective response, much maturity and self-awareness is needed so that you don't collude with the group. Ringer suggests that facilitators should not consider exploring in-depth psychodynamic approaches without first having developed strong facilitation and leadership skills (2002:243) – the potential clearly exists for the inexperienced facilitator to do more harm than good. However, there are some things you can put in place that help address these issues.

1 Good practice

This vital starting point forms the foundation for more direct intervention. Ensure you:

- contract and maintain effective boundaries;
- avoid authoritarian or laissez-faire leadership styles;
- use processes and approaches that encourage participation;
- create space for reflection and evaluation;
- plan seating to encourage interaction.

2 Methods and approaches

One proactive way of responding is to use facilitation techniques that directly contradict the basic assumption. In a dependent group, participative methods such as small-group discussion, fish-bowl or games will make the group the focus of the activity. In a pairing group, try using small groups or pairs work to break up pairing patterns. In a fight-flight group, approaches such as role-play can encourage the group to face, explore and discuss issues constructively.

In addition, you could design activities to highlight specific problems. In one church-based group I facilitated an experiential learning activity that highlighted the reluctance of people in the group to undertake a leadership role – one of the ways dependence manifested in this case. Members of the group acted as observers and facilitated reflection. Their observations initiated discussions on leadership that subsequently, over time, led to a growing willingness to take responsibility.

3 Direct intervention

Direct intervention can pose a dilemma for facilitators. Certain interventions – heavy-handedness, intellectualizing, over-spiritualizing – can re-enforce rather than address a group's dependence. However, withdrawal by facilitators can increase anxiety and be equally unproductive. Interventions should facilitate learning or encourage individual responsibility, not control or seek affirmation. Ensure you don't add to the problem by rescuing or 'mother hen' behaviours. Base verbal interventions on observation and be specific, neutral and non-accusatory. Use language the group is familiar with and encourage it to reflect and take responsibility.

In certain situations intervention is helpful and even essential. Humour used as a defence can be destructive to the group as well as the task, so may need challenging. Patterns of fight behaviour may need addressing for similar reasons. Although your interventions may be directed at an individual, they will need to be framed in a way that enables the whole group to take responsibility.

4 Explaining and exploring the basic assumption

For many groups, explicitly exploring the basic assumption could be threatening, confusing and may actually increase anxiety levels. In a dependent group it could emphasize the gap in knowledge between the facilitator and the group. In certain contexts, however, the explicit exploring of basic assumptions will provide key learning for the group – for example in a 'training for trainers' situation or where learning centres on group processes, facilitation or group dynamics. Here, exploring the group basic assumption can provide effective experiential learning.

It is clear that working with unconscious processes in groups is by no means simple or straightforward. Ringer (2002) proposes a metaphor of the group facilitator as 'artist', which helpfully emphasizes the symbolic nature of unconscious processes. The key issue is one of understanding and exploration rather than control. For the facilitator who will embrace uncertainty and the challenge of learning, growing and enhancing his or her self-awareness, the opportunity exists for a growing ability both to identify the basic assumption of a group and respond to it effectively, so that individuals and groups are empowered to reach their full potential.

For action and reflection

- What are your natural responses to conflict? Where do these come from? What aspects of these would you like to change?
- Think of a time when you have seen strong emotions expressed in a group context. How did you feel about it? How did you respond? How might an understanding of your responses inform your practice as a facilitator?
- Think of a time when you have been criticized and reflect on what was said and how it was communicated. What if anything could you learn from the criticism? Consider writing a letter to the person concerned – not to send but simply for your own development. Frame what you would say and how you would express yourself.

- Think of a recent or current conflict situation you have been involved with or are aware of. Use either mind-mapping or eco-mapping to explore it further.
- How do you respond to the material here regarding unconscious processes in groups? What evidence can you see of any of the basic assumptions in groups you have facilitated?

7

Beginnings and endings

JO WHITEHEAD

The person is always a nomad, journeying from threshold
to threshold, into ever different experiences. In each
new experience, another dimension of the soul unfolds.

(John O'Donohue)

Beginnings and endings are 'threshold' times, crossing places, liminal places in our experience where often emotions and feelings are heightened. As such they are incredibly important aspects of human experience. Jeff Lucas (2006:391) suggests that in preaching, 25 per cent of the preparation time should be spent on the beginning and the ending, and I believe the same principle applies in facilitation. In relation to this I find it helpful to think of beginnings and endings as processes rather than events.

Before the beginning

Many of the things that make for a successful facilitation experience happen in the unseen realm of preparation. This will look different depending on whether the context in which you are facilitating is known or unknown to you. In an unfamiliar context we will need to ensure we have sufficient information to plan effectively. This will include questions such as:

- How much space and what kind of space will you have?
- How many people will be there?
- What equipment is available and what will you need to bring with you?
- How many people are going to be there?
- What is the gender, age, cultural mix?
- Does anyone in the group have any additional needs?

- What are the expectations of those who have invited you and the members of the group?
- What information has been or needs to be sent out or given beforehand?

Communication before a gathering may or may not be up to you, depending on the situation, but it is helpful to provide as much information as possible so that people know what to expect, what the purpose of the gathering is, what they need to bring, the timings, how they find the venue and what they should do when they arrive. Clear communication can greatly assist in setting expectations and assisting participants in arriving relaxed, prepared and expectant rather than nervous, uncertain and anxious.

Your own preparation

Preparation picks up many of the issues we covered when we considered planning in Chapter 2. List the equipment you will need to take or make certain is available, and ensure you arrive with enough time to prepare and that you know where to find everything you need. I like to arrive with around an hour to spare if I'm facilitating somewhere new, so that I can ensure I have a good feel of the space available and that I'm set up in time to be able to focus on welcoming people as they arrive.

Another key aspect of preparation is prayer. I always find it helpful to pray for those who will be involved in a gathering – by name if I know them – and to ask God to help me to see them as he does. I try and use my imagination to think through how they might be feeling and what questions or issues they might be bringing with them.

If you have a tendency to get nervous, prayer can be particularly helpful. Encourage others to pray for you too. Other things that are helpful in managing nerves are ensuring that you are well prepared and well planned, and using meditation, centring or deep breathing to calm yourself.

If you are planning the first session of a new ongoing group, more time will need to be given to forming – in fact you may choose to spend the whole first session doing forming-focused activities, setting and establishing the group culture, getting to know one another and agreeing the purpose and intended outcomes of the group.

Starting well

Chapter 3 addresses most of the key issues around culture setting, but it is important to think through the information that participants will need at the beginning of a session. It may be helpful to find a visual way of clarifying the purpose of the gathering, perhaps ensuring it is visible on the first slide of a PowerPoint presentation or on a piece of flip-chart paper. Good beginnings will draw people in and focus attention. Avoid getting names wrong, using offensive humour or admitting you haven't prepared – all of these will undermine the confidence of the group. Prayer, a story, statistic, definition, question or fact can all focus attention helpfully at the beginning, or you may simply choose to start with introductions and a reminder of the purpose of the gathering.

Introductions

Even in a familiar context it is helpful to introduce yourself if some people present may not know you. Keep it short, simple and relevant to the context – for example, when facilitating a training session on a specific subject it may be helpful to say what experience you have in that particular area.

Normally I will ask the group members to introduce themselves if there is a chance some people don't know each other. It is easy to make assumptions about who knows who, but I have been in church groups where there are people present who I know by sight but not by name. With an unfamiliar group I tend to write down names to help me remember them and then try to use them fairly early on in the session. If you are facilitating in a context where you don't know the group and they don't know each other, name badges may be helpful.

In a bigger group full introductions may be too time-consuming, though it may be helpful to break people into smaller groups or give time for them to introduce themselves to a few people around them.

Some creative ways of doing introductions

- Ask people to say their names, where they come from and one other thing about themselves. Make sure people don't feel intimidated or put on the spot by asking for something astonishingly funny or outrageously personal. The idea is to help them relax, not put them under pressure. Go first yourself and model what you're looking for by sharing something simple and straightforward.

- Use alliteration – ask people to couple their name with an adjective starting with the same sound or the same letter. So, for example, I'm Jo and I'm jolly, jealous, jittery or jumpy (depending on the group I'm working with). This can also be quite a good way of helping you remember people's names!
- Use rhymes – this works similarly and is also helpful for remembering names. I'm Jo and I'm slow, I don't know, I'm in the flow . . .
- Ask people to think about and share what animal they would be and why.
- Have some simple questions on cards in a bowl and pass them round. Ask people to answer one question as part of introducing themselves.

The use and abuse of ice-breakers

Low-key ice-breakers can be useful at the beginning of a session. If they are to build confidence and assist the group to form, they need to be simple, inclusive and designed not to embarrass those involved. I have witnessed some very unhelpful ice-breakers – the worst generally involving invasion of personal space. Katrin remembers a training course she attended with people she didn't know where the ice-breaker involved the participants sitting on each other's laps, something she found physically and emotionally uncomfortable. Games that might work well on New Year's Eve with a group of friends are not normally the most effective and appropriate ice-breakers in facilitation contexts.

A good ice-breaker will not humiliate, embarrass or put people on the spot. Where possible you should join in and participate yourself – a good way of encouraging a sense of working and learning together. I find it helpful to try to make any ice-breakers flow with the theme of the session or gathering – in this way they can contribute to the purpose of what you are doing or be part of a layering of any learning that takes place.

Some low-cringe ice-breakers

- Ask the group to stand in alphabetical first-name order or calendar order of birthdays (not age or weight!). To make this trickier, ask them to do it without speaking, using only non-verbal communication and sign language.

- Collect postcards or other pictures so that you have a wide range of different images. Put them out on a table and ask people to choose a card that reminds them of something that happened to them during the previous week. This activity can be adapted to suit different themes and/or purposes or to evaluate a session. You could also use a collection of objects rather than pictures.

- Autograph Bingo involves putting a sheet together with a number of different categories or 'qualifications', such as 'Has a driving licence', 'Owns a pet', 'Is wearing socks', 'Was born in March'. Copy the sheet so each participant has one, then ask them to collect autographs around the room of people who fulfil the categories. Have a small prize for the first person to fill their sheet with signatures.

- Blob trees – <www.pipwilson.com> – are a good way of kicking off a session. A range of these are available online to help people identify where they are 'at'.

- Formulating a 'tweet' can be helpful, particularly for a group familiar with Twitter. Tweets have to be a maximum of 140 characters, which can give a helpful framework to a brief contribution.

- Use a child's jigsaw or some small jigsaws with only a few pieces. Hand out the pieces and ask the group to complete the puzzle collaboratively. Don't provide the picture.

- Use very corny jokes, such as those in Christmas crackers – enough for each person to have either the question or the punchline. Put these on separate cards and deal them out – participants should then find their matching questions or punchlines.

Welcoming new people or latecomers

It is important to acknowledge any latecomers, welcome them and – if the situation allows – bring them up to speed with the progress of the gathering. If a number of people arrive late this will be more of a challenge – you will need to decide how many times it is feasible to repeat the process. If I am expecting a number of latecomers I will often wait until everyone has arrived and take some time to welcome and reintroduce myself at that point. I will normally seek to start on time unless a large proportion of the group are delayed, in which case I tend to negotiate a slightly later starting time with those who are there.

Ending well

On holiday a couple of years ago I stayed in a hotel complex with very lush and well-kept grounds. On the way to the restaurant one morning my husband, Paul, and I spotted a hummingbird hovering around some plants near the entrance to one of the buildings in the complex. Struck by the bird's beauty we stopped to watch and saw that thebird was hovering around a tiny nest, attached to one of the plants. We watched the bird over a few days, but came down to breakfast one morning to find that the hotel had decided to 'update' the vegetation. The border had been stripped of plants, but the hummingbird was still there, searching in vain for its nest. For me this spoke really powerfully of the way we sometimes end or change things without realizing or acknowledging the personal investment individuals might have made in the thing we are closing. Something may have come to the end of its natural life, but simply removing it may cause a real sense of pain and loss to those involved – the implications of this need to be thought through and acknowledged.

Endings vary significantly and happen for all kinds of reasons. Some groups or projects will come to an end because of the completion of a specific task or because people are moving on to something new. Others may end because of changes in policy or focus. Some endings occur because something has not worked, because key people have moved on or because of something traumatic such as death, illness or relationship breakdown.

Because of these different reasons, and the varying perceptions individuals and groups may have, endings can be textured with emotional complexity. There can be many things going on at the same time. My experience of doing exit interviews with our BA students after three years in the group is that people have very different feelings about finishing. Some are excited about moving on to something new; some have invested significantly in relationships within the group and are grieving the potential loss of close contact with peers. Some are wrestling with uncertainty and anxiety about the next step; others are simply relieved that the three years are over. These different feelings significantly affect and inform the way we do endings with the group as a whole.

Practical approaches to endings

When it comes to endings, there needs to be continuity between the ending and the culture and style of what went before. Level of relationship in the group and the length of time they have been together – as well as the purpose and function of the group and the task–relationship balance – should inform what we do, as should the stage of development the group has got to and the level of personal investment made by individuals. Endings should give people space to recognize and acknowledge their feelings about the ending without becoming schmaltzy and sentimental.

'Now what?'

Hogan calls endings 'now what' sessions (2003:407), and the aspect of looking ahead to what might come next for individuals, the organization or the group as a whole is often an important aspect of the process. Evaluation may be an important part of this, as well as identifying hopes and dreams for the future.

Some endings may be about commissioning and have a sense of sending people out 'for' something. This may particularly be the case at the end of a course, where specific skills have been learnt or people have been equipped for a particular kind of ministry. These kinds of endings should recognize the sense of commissioning and sending, but should not be a 'sales pitch' approach, which can hype up enthusiasm without providing sufficient space for engagement with other dimensions of the ending.

Where people have been involved for a long time in something that takes them out of their normal context, there may be a sense of going back into the 'real world' and engaging with new challenges of life and ministry. These kinds of endings may also involve geographical or work-related moves, which will have implications for those involved.

Some ways of facilitating commissioning endings

- Ask participants to write a letter of encouragement to themselves that highlights what they have learnt, what they will take away and how they would like to apply their learning in the future. These should be put in envelopes and self-addressed. Gather these in at the end of the session and post out after a few weeks.

- Use stones to build a cairn to highlight significant lessons learnt and to put down markers for the future.
- Create bookmarks or postcards with an image and/or words that sum up a key aspect of the learning or sense of being together. These can be easily and relatively cheaply done online – for example, <www.vistaprint.co.uk>. Give these out to participants to take away with them.

Evaluation

An important aspect of endings may be evaluations and giving opportunity for people to feedback on the effectiveness of the group, what they have learnt and what might be done differently. In learning situations this is often done using a questionnaire, but less formal processes can be more relevant and engaging for a lot of groups. Seek evaluation methods that flow with the way the group has worked and the kinds of approaches used throughout. Evaluation should be focused around the aims and objectives you used in planning.

When introducing an evaluation, make it clear what the purpose is and how the information will be used. People need to know that what they are contributing is actually going to make a difference to your practice, the church or organization, plans for future groups or courses.

Some approaches to evaluation

- In a circle, ask participants to say one thing that is on their mind, either positive or negative, a question, opinion or reflection about the group. Make it clear that these contributions will be allowed to 'stand' without question, discussion or comment. Allow a few moments of silence beforehand for people to think, and afterwards pause for a moment before closing in prayer.
- Provide two sheets of flip-chart paper, one with a smiling and one with a frowning face. Put these on a large table – or tables – with pens. Ask people to write on the smiley sheet things they have found positive and helpful and on the frowning sheet things they would like to have been different or would change. Keep your

distance during the process so the participants don't feel watched as they respond.

- Using a clip-art image, photograph or drawn picture, create an evaluation tree, either on a large sheet of flip-chart paper or on individual A4 sheets. Participants should evaluate different aspects of the group experience by writing on the different parts:

  - the earth around the tree represents the environment;
  - the trunk represents the structure of the day or sessions;
  - the branches represent the activities and the experience of being in the group;
  - the leaves and/or fruit represent individual experience or learning.

  For added effect bring in a real tree – a small bay or similar – and ask people to write their feedback on small tags or labels they can then tie on the branches or trunk.

Letting go

In most endings there will be a sense of needing to leave some things behind. A key aspect of this is recognizing that loss is loss whatever it relates to. For many this might result in a kind of grieving process, and it is helpful to be aware of the stages of grief and so be prepared to respond to any that might manifest within the group.

- *Denial* – a sense of disbelief around the loss or the ending, which can result in avoidance of the issue.
- *Anger* – this might be expressed or suppressed and may be self-directed or directed against the facilitator or a person within or external to the group.
- *Bargaining* – this is about trying to recover what has been lost and may manifest in blaming or seeking to compromise or make deals about the future.
- *Depression* – this can be experienced within groups through withdrawal, lethargy, tears or sadness.
- *Acceptance* – usually happens when the above stages have been gone through. This is about coming to terms with the loss and planning to accommodate it.

When planning endings that we know are likely to involve a strong emotional dimension, it is important to bear these different stages in mind but also to recognize that they may not occur in this order or affect everyone in the group in the same way.

The emotional aspects of endings may be problematic for some participants. Some may believe their feelings are different from everyone else's and so feel isolated and find it hard to engage. Some may try to avoid the emotional aspects of endings either by opting out of a session altogether or by using a distancing coping mechanism to keep their emotions at bay. It is important not to make assumptions about what people are thinking and feeling, particularly if the group dynamic is strongly pushing in one particular direction. However you approach the ending, give people freedom to engage with the process as they wish and create enough space to acknowledge potentially diverse responses. Occasionally you may also need to identify an individual's particular needs and signpost them to further sources of support.

Some practical ways of creating space for exploring emotions and feelings can be found on pages 67–8.

Some rituals for letting go

- Writing a letter can be a helpful way of letting go of hurts, disappointments or negative feelings about a situation. These letters may not be sent but may be left in a box or sealed in an envelope to symbolize leaving the feelings behind.
- Give out small tubs of children's bubbles. Ask people to take some time to blow some bubbles and as they watch the bubbles float away, to think about the specific things they want to let go of.
- Make some small cards and luggage labels available and put a bin and a suitcase in the centre of the room. Encourage people to write down things they want to 'throw away' on the cards and things they want to 'take away' on the luggage labels. Then give space for people to put the throw-away things in the bin and tie the luggage labels on the case.

For action and reflection

- Map out some sample ways of introducing yourself that you could use in different contexts. Try and hone down your introductions to as few words as possible.

- Create some question cards that you could use with a group to help people share non-threatening information about themselves.
- Think of some endings you have been involved with. What were the strengths and weaknesses of the way these were facilitated?
- Create an evaluation tool to use with a group with which you work that is not word or writing based.

8

Facilitating informal worship

SIMON SUTCLIFFE

> Yet a time is coming and has now come when the true
> worshippers will worship the Father in the Spirit and in
> truth, for they are the kind of worshippers the Father seeks.
>
> (John 4.23)

Why would you need to facilitate informal worship?

For most Christians, worship forms the heart of the Christian community, so much so that many of our buildings are shaped to facilitate that worship, and much of the Church's resources and time are used to enable it to be as meaningful as possible for that community.

We also have to note the radical variety of worship on offer across and even within the different denominations. Some Christian communities prefer to use set liturgies (written prayers that people can follow either on paper or on a screen); others prefer a more extempore style. Some prefer band-led music and singing; others an organ. Some prefer to use songs written by contemporary writers; others hymns that have stood the test of time.

With such a rich menu of worship on offer in our churches it may be odd to ask how we might facilitate informal worship. What are the circumstances when this chapter might be of use? I will give two examples from my own ministry.

Cell church

One of the churches in which I ministered was a cell church (Potter, 2001) where most of the community met during the week in people's homes, as well as on Sunday morning or evening. The Sunday morning was contemporary band-led worship with a preacher. The evening worship was a more traditional style with the organ as the only instrument. The midweek groups met in members' living rooms and followed the guidance for running cell groups: they began with a welcome, had a time of worship, explored Scripture and looked at ways members might put their thoughts and discussions into practice over the coming week. This is sometimes referred to as the 'little wing' and 'big wing' of the church. The little wing consists of small – six to twelve people – worshipping communities meeting throughout the week; the big wing consists of the combined groups for a larger corporate act of worship.

The benefits of the small groups were numerous and many people enjoyed being part of them and leading them. The leaders of the groups would come together regularly for pastoral support and to identify any training needs. Often the most pressing issue was how to lead worship in a small group without the paraphernalia that usually accompanies Sunday worship. It seems that the only model many of us have for leading and participating in worship is the variety of styles offered in the big wing of the church (the larger, corporate, more formal acts of worship) as opposed to the little wing (the smaller, more intimate, informal ones).

Pioneering small communities

The second example of why we might want to explore the facilitation of informal worship comes from my experience as a pioneer in the Methodist tradition. There are now many resources for those called to pioneer ministry (Male, 2011), and it seems there is more work and thinking to be done in this vital ministry of the Church. Pioneer ministry, at its most basic, is the work of individuals and communities to find contemporary and relevant forms of church for the twenty-first century. The forms of these churches range as dramatically as the styles of worship found in more inherited forms. The Fresh Expressions website – <www.freshexpressions.org.uk> – gives a taste of the variety on offer. What is common to all of them is that they want to engage with those who don't consider themselves Christian and often find themselves in the company of those who have little or no Christian experience.

This means that pioneer communities need to think very carefully about how they introduce worship to those not used to it, and what form that worship will take. It is assumed that those who are attracted to fresh expressions of church are not attracted to, or are actively put off by, more inherited forms of church, and particularly the styles of worship offered there on a Sunday. This maybe an unfair assumption, but the result is that many new forms of church are doing worship in very different ways. So worship in a pioneering context, particularly in the early days of forming a new community, is often informal.

Experimenting

One of my first experiments in this area was forming a community that met in a village hall one Saturday a month. A team would load a van with sofas (from our homes), lamps, rugs and candles! In the hall we would set up a coffee bar and arrange the sofas, rugs, chairs and tables in such a way that meant groups of people could chat in small groups. In another part of the hall we created a prayer labyrinth (or Stations of the Cross in Lent), and the final area was an area for craft and art materials. We had an acoustic set where musicians would play contemporary Christian music at various points in the night. The whole thing lasted about three hours and people were free to choose what they wanted to do and when. The only real fixed point in the night was when a guest was interviewed about the work of social justice they were currently engaged in.

This informal act of worship on a Saturday night differed very much from the more formal ones I engaged with on the following Sunday morning. There was no 'order of service' and nobody directed people from the front as to what they were doing next. The onus was on individual worshippers both to participate in the worshipping experience and help shape it for others. Worship like this might not be to everyone's liking, particularly those who find traditional Sunday worship enriching; but for those called to pioneer ministry it is highly likely that facilitating informal worship will be part of the job description.

This chapter should be useful to those who are leading small groups as part of a larger church and for those seeking to form new worshipping Christian communities, although the issues will also be relevant to any who plan, facilitate and lead more formal acts of worship.

Worship in tension

In order to explore how we might facilitate informal worship, we first need to identify our aim. What we are hoping to achieve? There are clearly many ways to answer that question but I want to offer a simple response born out of two assumptions. The first is that God is omnipresent – he is all around us and in between us. The second is that human beings have the capacity to experience alterity – a sense of otherness. It is this capacity that enables us to experience awe, wonder and amazement. In any act of worship I am hoping that people *connect* with the ever-present God in such a way that they are drawn into a narrative that is larger than their own story. That might be an emotional response – a real sense of wonder and amazement; or a cerebral response – a reasoned understanding that the individual is part of a big picture.

Holding the space

The way we facilitate that kind of informal worship is to *hold open the space* long enough for people to begin to connect. That space is both the physical environment and the *head/heart-space* people need to make associations between their actuality and the divine reality. When that happens then worship has happened. Jonny Baker begins to explore this in the first part of his book, *Curating Worship* (2010), and then goes on to interview practitioners – or curators – of worship from the *alt. worship* scene. Many of the experiences and themes to be drawn out of that book will be useful alongside this more general introduction to facilitating informal worship. But the question remains: how do we keep open the space for encounter?

I want to suggest that we do so by holding in tension opposing forces that – were we to allow one to overwhelm the other – would collapse the space so that the act either ceases to be worship or ceases to be informal. To facilitate informal worship is to hold open the space, and we do that by being attentive to those things that might invade it.

Order and chaos

Holding the tension between order and chaos is probably the most difficult task for a facilitator of informal worship. If you arrive with an order of service and script to work from then it will feel much more formal, even if the setting is informal. In fact the reason many small group leaders struggle with informal worship is because they try to recreate large worship on a smaller scale. Equally, if there is no order then the whole thing can be confusing and feel a bit like a circus, where different acts perform at seemingly random moments. This can be particularly true when the worship is aimed at families and children.

One way of maintaining the balance is to decide on a number of fixed points. So for an hour's worship you might want three fixed moments that act like markers – wherever you are during the worship, you can make your way back to one of them or move on to the next. It might be a poem, listening to a piece of music, an interview with someone, a craft activity and so on. In order for it not to feel like an order of service, the facilitator must then relinquish control of the moments in between those fixed points. So if, for instance, a poem is read and the facilitator wants to pursue a conversation in response to it, he or she must frame a question such as, 'What did it remind you of?' or offer a method. I use a wow, ouch and hmmm method:

- What made you think 'Wow – I like that'?
- What made you think 'Ouch – I don't like that'?
- What made you think 'Hmmm – I need to think about that'?

For experienced worship practitioners this can be very difficult and disconcerting. Generally worship leaders prefer to have clear outcomes. They often have a message they want the worshippers to hear but informal worship asks worshippers to shape that message and outcome for themselves, hence facilitators have less of a contribution to make to the overall theme; instead they are busy holding open the space between order and chaos.

Challenges

This does leave two difficulties for the facilitator. First, what if no one participates? There is a danger that some acts of informal worship are a bit like a school disco: lots of people present but nobody wants to join in! This is especially the case if people are asked to do something that is unusual to them (page 99). If that is the case it is likely that the facilitator has chosen a style of worship unsuitable for the worshippers present – just as in formal acts of worship some styles are more suitable to particular types of worshippers than others.

The second problem is the opposite of the first: the worship is either taken over by a few individuals or driven by a particular agenda.

Chapters 4 and 6 introduce a range of tools that might be of use, particularly when dealing with dysfunctional groups. However, the problem of driven agendas is much more difficult to deal with. I have sat in many acts of small group worship and heard comments and prayers or seen artistic responses that are either offensive to particular groups of people or even heretical!

If the facilitator holds the space he or she can either move the group on to the next fixed point (or take it back to another one – 'Let's read that poem again and see what else it tells us') or allow the difficult moment to pass in the hope that another worshipper will contribute in a more positive light. Either way it probably requires some pastoral care outside the act of worship itself.

Even when the worship does stray into the offensive and heretical, it is important to remember that worship is only a snapshot of where a particular community is at a given time. I'm horrified at some of my past sermons! But if worship enables people to connect their story with the story of God, we are inevitably going to find ourselves in complex and sometimes uncharted territory.

Relevance and the inaccessible

The facilitator of informal worship must hold the space between what is relevant to the community and what is inaccessible. This is primarily about language and concepts but can also be about activities. For example, most adults over 30 are unlikely to sing publicly unless they are in one of three occasions: a concert, a football match or the karaoke. It then feels awkward for them to sing together in a small group in a living room or café. Equally, the language we use can often be a barrier to people's participation. When we ask people to pray, do they know what we are asking them to do? But at the same time, a facilitator is hoping that the worshipper enters into a much deeper sense of self and the divine. In that sense it is bound to be *unknowable*.

I once asked a group of children and adults a set of questions after watching a short clip from a film. I asked the adults how they recognized God's Kingdom in the world and I asked the children what they could do to make the world a better place. I discovered that the adults struggled with their question but the children loved wrestling with theirs. In the end the adults chose to answer the question I set for the children rather than the one I had asked them.

The language of *Kingdom* meant that the adults could not participate because I had not helped them understand more fully what I meant by Kingdom.

In another example a child told his parent that he loved the new church because they never used the Bible. This of course wasn't true! The facilitator simply used phrases like 'There is an ancient poem that goes, "In the beginning was the Word . . ."' or 'This is a story I remember about a man who had two sons . . .'.

It is clear that the language, concepts and activities used have the power to enable or disable worship. The facilitator of informal worship, particularly with groups new to Christian faith, must be aware of that power and ensure that groups not only have a good understanding of what is expected of them but also of the jargon and theological language that might be used. However, the facilitator should also be careful not to rob the worship of a sense of mystery and alterity. Not every song, poem or piece of art needs to be explained, and there are certain elements of worship, such as the sacraments, that are sometimes better experienced than understood. It is usually experience of facilitating informal worship and familiarity with the group that helps the facilitator discern when to explain and when to leave alone.

Clutter and the mundane

Holding the space between clutter and the mundane asks the facilitator to be attentive to the physical space. In most forms of Sunday worship the space is already dictated and bears the signs, symbols and equipment necessary for the act of worship. Most acts of informal worship, on the other hand, happen outside of church buildings. This can often present a challenge for facilitators – whether to use the space as it is or transform it into something else.

I would suggest that the space used for worship needs to look different from how it was and will be again. So whether in a living room, village hall or café, permission ought to be sought to add to and take away from the space. The purpose is to try to create an environment for the worshipping community that is conducive to the style of worship offered. It might be that a focal piece is created in the centre of the room or, in larger spaces, that different parts of the room are decorated or furnished in particular ways. The needs of the community are obviously essential – there is no point providing 20 beanbags for a group of people who would struggle to sit on them. As it is also very useful to try stimulating other senses, essence and oil burners, music and ambient lighting might also be considered.

Technology

A note ought to be made here on the use of technology in informal worship. Computers, screens and projectors are commonplace now in many Christian communities, and if yours does not have one there is a good chance they can borrow one. These are particularly useful in larger spaces when you want many people to see the same thing. In smaller settings, particularly in someone's home, it might be possible to use the host's television (many newer televisions have a VGA input), so that people can see the same thing. For those who are more technologically aware there is the possibility of using social media in worship. The facilitator can present questions and/or see feedback through a variety of social media platforms. It is also becoming increasingly common for people to have their Bibles and other resources on their mobile phones or other digital devices. This can give individuals more flexibility as they find passages, poems, songs or pictures on their devices to share with the rest of the group.

So a space can be transformed and made to look and feel different through a variety of sensory material and using technology. The danger is that the space can soon look like an Aladdin's cave that becomes a distraction rather than an aid to worship. Too many focal points or one that is too large in a small room can feel very claustrophobic. Equally, being overwhelmed by smell or sound is offputting. Technology often involves wires that can also make a space look uninviting (and even dangerous), so care must be taken in what equipment is used, where it is set up and how it is operated. The most difficult problem to overcome with respect to a cluttered worship space is often in people's homes when there are too many people for the size of the room. This can result in extra chairs forced into spaces that either block other people's view or leave some feeling exposed. If that is the case then celebrate the growth of the group and either relocate to a larger space or separate it in two and grow! This might need some pastoral sensitivity but it is a good problem to have.

Final thoughts

In this chapter I have suggested that a facilitator of informal worship hopes to maintain the tension between order and chaos. This will ensure the worship remains informal and yet still has a direction of travel. The facilitator will also want to ensure that the worship is suitably understood without depriving it of a sense of *otherness* – this will allow people to participate fully in the worship and leave room for an encounter with God. Finally, a facilitator will want to transform the space so that it becomes more than ordinary – extra-ordinary – but not so much so that it becomes a distraction to those trying to worship. If facilitators can successfully retain these tensions, they will hold open the space for encounter to be possible.

Any practitioner will know that holding that space is difficult and mainly a matter of trial and error. Those things that work with one group might not with another. Those things that work with one group in a particular setting might not do so well with the same group in another. And sometimes a group just finds it difficult to worship. I would advise any facilitator to gain regular feedback from worshippers and spend time understanding the dynamics and principles behind liturgy and more formal forms of worship (Earey, 2002). This will help to develop their ability, but in the end, worship cannot be forced. The facilitator can simply hold open the space and trust that the worshipper and God will do the rest.

For action and reflection

- In your context, when might informal worship be more appropriate than formal styles?
- How do you feel about having less control over the worshipping experience than you might in more traditional forms of worship?
- If you are a practitioner – do you regularly receive feedback on your worship (formal or informal)? Could you produce a simple feedback form that you could give out to a few individuals before worship?
- Try to keep a journal of different worship events you attend and/or lead. Note the style, the high and low points and your reactions to the worship as a whole.
- If you lead or attend a small group, ask the group if they can experiment with different ideas in leading collaborative and participative

worship. Spend some time – twice a year – having a discussion about what has been helpful and what less so.

- If your church has seeker groups or introduction to faith groups, see if you can facilitate worship with them. Try holding the space in relevant and accessible ways.

- If you belong to a small group that usually meets in one place, why not 'go on tour' and try using different spaces for informal worship (café, pub, meeting room, other houses and so on)?

9

Facilitating meetings

JO WHITEHEAD

> Coming together is a beginning; keeping together is progress;
> working together is success. (Henry Ford)

Meetings often appear to make up the texture of life within churches and Christian organizations. We meet to coordinate, plan, address business issues, make decisions, consult, share ideas or information, pray, worship, support or supervise. To a certain extent any get-together of people could be loosely described as a meeting. However, this chapter focuses more specifically on those meetings that are more task focused, meetings that could be described as 'a gathering of individuals collaborating with the interests of the organization at its core, for a scheduled amount of time' (Peberdy and Hammersley, 2009:xii).

There sometimes appears to be an unhelpful separation between the so-called 'spiritual' aspects of church and the more practical and managerial aspects of ministry. My favourite biblical 'manager' is Nehemiah, who motivates and leads God's people in rebuilding the walls of Jerusalem. Nehemiah seems adept at exercising leadership and management gifts to get the work done. He negotiates safe passage to Jerusalem (Nehemiah 2.7) and assesses the task and what is needed (2.13–15). He motivates people to join in the work and to work effectively and collaboratively (2.17—3.32). People are named individually and individual contributions to the work are valued and recognized. When discouragement and attack come he encourages those who are building and organizes strategies to protect them (4.12–23). He engenders a sense of community and joint enterprise, gathering people at key times and working for justice within the community (5.1–18). All this is accomplished through and underpinned by prayer, fasting, responsiveness to and dependence on God.

As we consider some very practical aspects of meetings – how to plan, facilitate meetings, be a facilitative participant – Nehemiah gives a helpful model of how to ground our practice in relationship with God, through prayer, responsiveness and wisdom.

To meet or not to meet?

In considering the issue of meetings, a helpful starting point is to ask whether it is actually essential to meet at all. Some meetings become such an established part of church culture that this question is rarely asked and they become taken for granted, though their purpose is no longer clear and certainly not articulated. In seeking to accomplish tasks there can be great advantages in meeting face-to-face. Communication can be clearer and personal responses and reactions can be conveyed through facial expression and body language as well as through what is said. Sometimes face-to-face conversations can generate a creativity and momentum that may take a lot longer if people are communicating by phone or, say, by email or social media. Face-to-face meetings can also help establish and grow a sense of team and belonging for those involved, which can result in greater ownership of decisions made and increased willingness to take responsibility for implementing them.

However, in some cases, for cost- or time-saving reasons, it may be helpful to consider communicating by email or holding a telephone or Skype conference.

Planning meetings

As I have emphasized already, it is vital that the person facilitating the meeting – and all those taking part – have a clear understanding of its purpose and intended product or outcomes. Once these have been clearly established they will form the foundation and focus for the planning that takes place. They will also provide helpful steer during the meeting itself to ensure things stay on track.

Who should be there?

The purpose and outcomes may be agreed collaboratively or be the responsibility of an individual or smaller group, but once clear, the next step is to identify who should be involved. There may be different rationales for different individuals' involvement. Some may be there because of their role, position or responsibility. Some may attend in a representative capacity. Others may be invited because of particular knowledge, skills or expertise. Ensure that people are only involved who need to be, bearing in mind that at times you may choose to invite someone for their own benefit as part of a learning or development process, rather than for what they may specifically contribute.

Structuring an agenda

The word agenda literally means 'things to be done' (Peberdy and Hammersley, 2009:101). Agendas are important because they provide the meeting with a focus and a structure. They may include items for information, discussion, consultation, decision, ratification and review (Adirondack, 1998:38).

People will design agendas in different ways. In part this will depend on the amount of business to be worked through, the complexity of the issues, the degree of formality of the meeting and any potential legal requirements. Hence some meetings – of charity trustees or directors for example – will be required by law to keep signed minutes of meetings, for which a very structured agenda will be essential. Other meetings may have a very informal agenda, which may be in the form of a loose plan, held by the facilitator. I would argue that even in the most informal contexts, some way of clarifying what the meeting is going to cover and consider is helpful in enabling people to prepare and participate meaningfully. In a very informal context the agenda may be agreed collaboratively at the beginning of the meeting.

Some things to consider when planning an agenda:

- The amount of material to be covered – check that it is realistic. Be clear about the finishing time and plan only what is possible in the time. It is demoralizing to get only halfway through an agenda.
- The order of business – recognize that particularly in the evening, the later it gets the less productive most people become. Some content of the meeting may be determined by expectations or legal requirements of items to be covered. A review of the previous meeting's minutes will generally be one of the earliest items, and most agendas will finish with 'Any Other Business'.

- Whether to put in guidelines on how much time to give each item – some indication can be helpful, although simply identifying whether the focus is information, agreement or discussion will do this.
- The way the agenda is numbered – this will depend on the context and level of formality. Keep things simple unless a complex numbering system is required for legal reasons.
- Any additional information needed to support agenda points, such as reports, additional reading or policies – these should be sent out in advance of the meeting, preferably with the agenda, so people have time to read through and think about them.
- It may be relevant to put names against specific items – this is if you wish someone to take responsibility for leading a particular section or providing information.
- Keep items for discussion open in terms of the way they are expressed – this is normally helpful, rather than revealing pre-set ideas or controversial viewpoints.

Preparing yourself for the meeting

Once the agenda has been sent out there are various things you can do to prepare. Look through it and think how much time will be needed on each area – try to be realistic and plan for some slippage. Peberdy and Hammersley (2009) suggest developing a second agenda for yourself as facilitator – here you rank the items in order of importance (rather than running order), to highlight priorities: what the meeting must achieve and what decisions must be made. This can help if time runs short, particularly if you are not a completer-finisher. This will ensure conversations and discussions don't simply continue indefinitely without any firm ways forward being established.

We have already explored the area of culture setting extensively in Chapter 3, and in your preparation you will need to plan the different aspects of the space you will use, including seating arrangements, refreshments, equipment and atmosphere. You will also need to consider provision for anyone attending who may have additional needs or requirements and think through any particular roles and dynamics that may be part of the meeting. For example, is someone going to take minutes? Are there any existing or potential tensions, conflicts or issues that may need particularly sensitive handling?

Consider the processes you will use. Many meetings focus virtually solely on discussion, but consider creating texture and variety within the meeting by using different approaches. Some suggestions are given later in this chapter; others can be found in Chapter 5.

Facilitating meetings

If you are chairing a meeting, ensure you arrive at a time that allows you to set up, get ready and be prepared to welcome and greet people.

Think about the meeting and consider carefully what you are seeking to communicate at the beginning – for example, whether welcomes, introductions, ice-breakers, social time and/or prayer will be relevant to your context. If you don't know everyone, sketch the room and write people's names next to where they are sitting so that you can write them in by name as opportunity arises. Ensure that you communicate and present material clearly and effectively during the meeting. Signpost to other resources and draw others in if necessary.

The facilitator should move through the agenda clearly, while allowing space for healthy and honest discussion of relevant issues. Brookfield and Preskill (1999:3) emphasize how 'by giving the floor to as many different participants as possible, a collective wisdom emerges that would have been impossible for any of the participants to achieve on their own'. Highlight decisions to be made and ensure that agreement is reached and action points noted. Firmness and sensitivity will be needed to maintain the boundaries of the group; challenge any inappropriate behaviour or contributions. Ensure that all have opportunity to contribute, and maintain and refocus attention as necessary.

Another important issue to consider when chairing is working within your values. If you are consulting, make sure it is genuine consultation. If you are encouraging participation, make sure it is genuinely participatory. However powerless you may feel at times, the position of facilitator or chair is a powerful one, and it is important to avoid manipulation, bullying or using personal position or charisma to push through your own agendas. If you hold a position of power in the church and have personal power in addition to this, there may be a temptation to seek to use this to get your own way. However, in the longer term this is not an effective way to lead meetings. Others will begin to wonder why they are there if they just appear to be rubber-stamping decisions you have already made, and they will be reluctant to implement decisions made when their views are not respected.

Some suggestions for keeping to time

Try the following (adapted from Peberdy and Hammersley 2009:180):

- summarize, conclude and suggest moving on;
- suggest an issue be 'parked' until the next meeting;
- suggest an issue be dealt with by a subgroup if necessary and returned to at the next meeting;
- suggest an extension for the meeting.

Encouraging participation

Even when we recognize the importance of representation and seek to avoid being tokenistic, we need to ensure that the processes we use encourage participation and enable all those present to be involved. Mary, the chair of a Christian youth project, went to great lengths to include young people in the management committee and expressed her frustration to me about their lack of commitment and contributions. Although they seemed interested, the two youth representatives said virtually nothing in any meeting and were reluctant to take any responsibility. Mary was committed to helping them be more involved but struggled to see how. In discussion it emerged that the style of the meetings was extremely formal, influenced by Mary's business background and desire to do things right. The style of expression and vocabulary used in the agendas and other paperwork would have been difficult for most adults to understand, and on reflection Mary realized that the focus on debate, critique and discussion probably felt quite alienating and threatening to the young people. She began to meet with them before the meetings to chat through what was going to happen, and worked hard at simplifying documentation and using simpler, more creative and participative processes. Unsurprisingly the young representatives showed a huge rise in enthusiasm and commitment and it wasn't long before they were much more actively involved.

Encouraging a positive attitude

Some meetings can become swamped with negativity, and for facilitators facing this kind of challenge, appreciative enquiry (Whitney and Trosten-Bloom, 2003) can be a helpful approach. Appreciative enquiry has been described as 'solving problems by looking at what's going right' – <www.mindtools.com>. It focuses on looking at things within organizations that are going well and building on the positives. Once a problem or issue has been identified, appreciative inquiry works in four stages.

1 *Discover* – look at things that have worked well in the past or are working well currently. Get as many people as possible involved in telling stories about them or about things they have appreciated. Collate and reflect on the responses received.
2 *Dream* – think about and imagine what might be in the future. Think about how you can build on the strengths you have identified and generate ideas of what you could do or what might happen in the future.
3 *Design* – build on the things identified in the dream phase; look at the practicalities needed to bring the dream to fulfilment.
4 *Deliver* – this is the implementation phase. Keeping the dream in mind, plan and implement the key changes needed to make the design a reality.

Being a facilitative participant

Even if we are not chairing a meeting ourselves there are ways of being a facilitative member or participant that can support the rest of the group, the facilitator and the process. This doesn't mean hijacking control of a meeting being led by someone else! Here are some suggestions.

- Be prepared. Read through materials in advance. Do some thinking and extra research if possible. Consult with others if appropriate about what is going to be talked about but ensure you don't collude. If it helps, make some notes and take these with you.
- Be a listener. Don't spend the whole time framing what you are going to contribute – really focus on what others are saying. You may find it helpful to write things down so your mind doesn't wander.
- Think carefully about what you are going to say and then try to communicate clearly and coherently. Try not to interrupt or ride roughshod over others in the group. Be concise, don't waffle, and own your own opinions rather than speak on behalf of others.

- Respect other perspectives even if you don't agree with them. Seek to be calm and measured in your responses and don't use put-downs, offensive humour or other point-scoring techniques.

Notes and recordings

It is usually helpful to have notes or minutes as a record of what has happened, of discussions and of any decisions made. There are a range of styles, but the most important thing is that they should be clear and suited to the context. They are useful for those who were present but also for those who were not. They therefore need to be full enough for someone to follow who wasn't there, without being a lengthy or over-detailed description of the meeting. In this regard it is helpful to summarize, use bullet points and refer to other documentation rather than duplicating – reports or presentations used in the meeting can be attached rather than summarized.

If you are taking minutes you need to have enough awareness of what is going on to take notes in an informed and clear way, without slanting the minutes to reflect what you wish had been said. It will be helpful at times to clarify what others have said so that you show you have listened and correctly understood their views – for example, 'If I understood you rightly, you said . . .' Use annotations to highlight who contributed or to emphasize action points.

It may be helpful to ensure that decisions are identified before the end of the meeting and that action points are clearly articulated and agreed.

Sometimes wisdom will be needed as to what is and is not included in the minutes. If sensitive pastoral information or confidential matters are being discussed, for example, there will need to be agreement on what is written down. At times it may be necessary for some to leave the meeting for particularly sensitive agenda items or if there is a conflict of interest.

Some creative ways of texturing meetings

Post-it note pyramid

This is a good approach to exploring an issue or engaging in decision-making. Participants note issues, priorities or arguments on individual post-its. Either individually or in pairs they then establish a hierarchy of importance, with one post-it (the most important thing) at the top, then two below (the next most important), then three and so on. By looking at the different pyramids around the room you can see what patterns emerge, where there is common ground and where differences. The pyramids can be photographed and included in the minutes.

Visual mapping

Mapping a discussion visually can help focus and engage participants. Sibbet (2010:34–5) suggests several approaches:

- *posters* – using single, punchy images, for example a small drawing on a flip-chart page;
- *lists* – linear sequences of information;
- *clusters* – presenting information in chunks on a page;
- *grids* – more complex, usually using rectangles and boxes to categorize;
- *diagrams* – linking information in branching patterns;
- *drawings* – illustrating a point or issue;
- *mandalas* – organizing everything around a central point, usually in a circle.

You don't have to be artistic to do this but it helps to have clear handwriting. If this isn't you, practise, or enlist someone else in the group.

These kinds of approaches are likely to take more time but really can assist in maintaining concentration and increasing participation. Simple processes, such as breaking into pairs, can make all the difference in ensuring everyone is heard, if you have some very quiet members within the group. You will need to consider before the meeting what materials you need and what is going to be best suited.

After meetings

Follow-up is a really important aspect of the effectiveness of meetings. Particularly if we are busy we can tend simply to breathe a sigh of relief when a meeting is finished and move on, or get caught up in the business of the next meeting or demand on our time. We may find that the things we got excited or motivated about have got swamped in other 'stuff'. Ensure minutes are sent out promptly so people are clear as to their memory of events and don't receive them the day before the next meeting!

If you tend to put things off, use a highlighter to note on the minutes action points where your name appears and to remind you of responsibilities to which you have agreed. Also make a note in your diary or 'to do' list so they don't get overlooked and forgotten. Check for information that others need so that you maintain an awareness of the bigger picture. Consider how these minutes might inform the agenda for the next meeting. It may be helpful to begin to think already about the next agenda – the cyclical nature of many meetings becomes evident here.

For action and reflection

- In what meetings are you regularly involved? Map these out, listing the positives and negatives of how they function and your role in them.
- If you are responsible for certain meetings in your church or organization, take time to revisit their purpose and effectiveness.
- Next time you are involved in a meeting, take the role of participant-observer. Be aware of how the meeting is led and facilitated and how those present contribute or not. Observe your own attitudes, thoughts, feelings and contributions and consider how these assist – or do not – the effectiveness of the meeting.

10

Facilitating learning and reflection

JO WHITEHEAD

> I am still learning. (Michelangelo)

> If a question can't become a quest (vision quest, grail quest, hope quest) then it's not worth asking.
> (Leonard Sweet et al., 2003:247)

Learning and reflection happen in a whole range of ministry contexts, from relatively formal teaching and preaching, Bible study and prayer groups to informal conversation, activities and relationships. Some of these experiences will be planned and structured; others will emerge more organically and unexpectedly as we live, work, play, worship and grow together. I see both learning and reflection as 'whole person' processes that we should be embracing ourselves as well as facilitating for others.

> To learn in the hands of the living God will challenge our sense of identity. It will take us, with a God who is 'both the ancient of days and the eternal child', into a lifelong seeking after understanding that brings us to the limit of our comprehension. (Ward, 2005:4)

Facilitative approaches to learning

Some more traditional models of learning utilize a 'banking' approach (Freire, 1972), which sees facilitators as 'experts' and participants as the beneficiaries of their knowledge, wisdom and experience. Learners are seen as empty vessels to be filled and are, by and large, passive recipients of information. This passivity often results in dependency on the facilitator and a consumerist approach to learning. Although there will be times when you will need to impart or communicate information to support learning and development, the banking approach has little to recommend it from a facilitative perspective.

Experiential approaches to learning are more congruent with facilitative styles. These see the learner at the centre of learning experiences and engaging actively in them. Research has shown that adults learn best when they are learning from experience, can share their experience as part of the process, are learning collaboratively with others and really understand the purpose of what is being learnt (Sheal, 1989). These values fit well with facilitation principles, encouraging approaches that seek to be engaging, empowering, purposeful and practical.

In learning contexts we need to focus on process (the learning journey) as much as product (the content to be learnt). The experiential learning cycle (adapted from Kolb, 1984), although very simple, is a helpful starting point in thinking about learning journeys, although I would emphasize that it needs to be seen as an ongoing spiral rather than a closed circle, and that the complexity of different situations needs to be taken into account (see Figure 11).

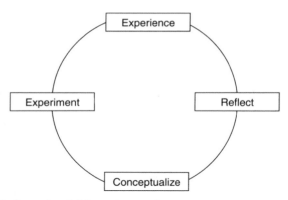

Figure 11 Experiential learning cycle

Approaches to reflection

This cycle also forms the basis of reflective practice and is the foundation for the pastoral cycle, the most commonly used approach to theological reflection. Reflection has been described as 'the art of deliberately slowing down our habitual processes of interpreting our lives to take a closer look at the experience and at our frameworks for interpretation' (Killen and de Beer, 1994:x). This definition helpfully emphasizes how reflection not only encourages us to look

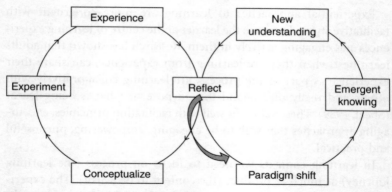

Figure 12 Double-loop learning

at our lives and the world around us but at our own preconceived ideas and worldviews – the ways we interpret and make sense of all we experience. This is reflected in the concept of double-loop learning, which extends the experiential learning cycle to show how the learning process potentially challenges and changes learners' existing paradigms – their ways of seeing and understanding the world (adapted from Brockbank and McGill, 1998:45). Brockbank and McGill emphasize the need for facilitators to create sufficient reflective space and be comfortable with the expressions of emotion that are necessary to motivate and generate double-loop learning (see Figure 12).

In the busyness and activism of life (perhaps particularly church life), incorporating reflection into our gatherings is vitally important. Reflection can enhance church business meetings and decision-making processes as well as being a key part of worship and learning. Whatever the context, it will be helpful to bear the following principles in mind.

Reflection is corporate as well as individual

Reflection is often perceived as a personal activity that happens in solitude, but the most effective theological reflection arguably happens in a group context (Green, 1990). Affirming corporate aspects of reflection helps challenge the culture of individualism that appears to pervade society and the Church. Language used in regard to *personal* faith, the making of a *personal* commitment and having a *personal* relationship with God appears to contradict Kingdom values, which emphasize community and connectedness. Although we may need to create space for individual reflective space within corporate processes, engaging in reflection with others often results in a collective wisdom emerging as group members contribute different insights, perspectives and experiences.

Reflection is exploratory

It is important to find a place to stand from which to undertake reflection. Killen and de Beer suggest three potential standpoints, two of which form opposite ends of a spectrum. The standpoint of certitude (1994:5) emphasizes absolute truth and a sense of certainty that the person reflecting understands how God is at work and what should be done in response. This standpoint focuses primarily on Scripture and Christian tradition but may fail to take into account the cultural lenses through which we inevitably read and interpret the theological tradition or biblical material. At the opposite end of the spectrum, the standpoint of self-assurance (1994:13) rejects the resources of Christian tradition in favour of immediate personal experience, feelings and thoughts. This approach uses the tradition only to support what the individual reflecting thinks or feels, rather than allowing it to speak powerfully and with integrity into human experience.

In the middle of these two, and holding them in creative tension, Killen and de Beer propose a 'standpoint of exploration' (1994:16), where questions predominate to encourage genuine conversation between experience and the wisdom of the Christian tradition. This place of exploration calls for robust self-awareness in terms of our own worldviews. The standpoint of exploration is not necessarily a comfortable place as it involves engaging rigorously with some of the questions, tensions and challenges that emerge when our experience doesn't seem to match with our understanding of the Christian tradition. But this healthy wrestling arguably leads to a greater depth of engagement with the issues being explored and a greater sense of ownership of those things being learnt.

This sense of exploration, I believe, provides a helpful way to understand reflective processes as we recognize that different individuals and groups will find themselves in different places on the spectrum between certainty and self-reliance.

Reflection as conversation

Another way of understanding this sense of exploration is to see theological reflection as conversation (Killen and de Beer, 1994; Ballard and Pritchard, 2006). Davis highlights the Latin root of the word conversation, which 'implies a place of habitation, a home where those "in conversation" share a common life'. He contrasts this with the word discussion, which has a very different foundation, being derived from a Latin word, *discutere*, that carries with it a sense of dashing something to pieces (2002:18). Facilitating these kinds of conversations can be challenging when people hold very strong and deeply held views, but good boundaries, an agreed group contract and sensitive facilitation skills will assist in encouraging conversations in which different contributions are listened to, respected and valued. This will involve the development of interpersonal skills such as owning what is said through the use of the 'I' voice, listening, clarifying and coping with conflict and difference (Killen and de Beer, 1994:78). In contexts where we are seeking to listen to what the Holy Spirit might be saying, wisdom and skill will be needed by facilitators to allow different voices to be heard and valued. Discernment will also be vital in holding a safe space where different contributions can be weighed and owned to see patterns and insights emerge.

Reflection and theological rigour

Pattison has identified the danger of trying to engage in practical theology without the necessary tools and resources, using the 'bricks without straw' metaphor from Exodus (in Woodward and Pattison, 2000), where the enslaved Israelites were forced to make clay bricks without the straw that would normally help the clay to bind. Although I believe all Christians should be theologians, in that they are seeking to make sense of and apply their faith (Green, 1990), in today's culture, where biblical literacy is on the decline, you may find yourself having to bring theological resources into the reflective process. It is not that we should be expected to have all the answers, but a commitment to facilitating theological reflection involves a personal process of learning and growing in the wisdom and insights of the Christian tradition. This will involve an understanding of the context of different aspects of the tradition and of Scripture.

Whole-person reflection

Effective reflection is assisted by understanding that we bring the whole of ourselves to the process, with our histories, feelings, responses, circumstances, current challenges and the ordinary aspects of our everyday lives. Spiritually our reflection should be soaked in prayer, worship and study. Theological reflection, if undertaken well, has the potential to help us grow significantly in our faith. Indeed, Killen and de Beer would go further and claim that,

> Without authentic theological reflection we Christians cannot achieve the personal maturity and integrity appropriate to us. Theological reflection that involves heart and mind, consciousness and activity, provides a discipline in the life of faith. It enables us to integrate seemingly irreconcilable realms of activity and knowledge in our lives.   (1994:15)

Deep learning and reflection

My hope and desire in facilitating learning and reflection in ministry contexts is that the experience will be transformative in terms of people's lives and their relationship with God. This can be seen as the difference between head knowledge and heart knowledge. The term 'learning by heart' traditionally suggests memorization and rote learning – a predominantly surface approach. True *heart learning* incorporates a biblical understanding of the heart as the centre of the inward life – the source of values, attitudes, perceptions, desires, affections, understanding, reasoning, imagination, conscience, purpose and faith.

This kind of 'deep learning' (Marton and Säljö, 1976) is about the quality of what is learnt rather than the quantity. It relates to the way people understand principles and meaning rather than memorizing facts and figures – how they connect what they are learning and apply it to life. When people learn something at a deep level, it is processed internally so that it becomes part of who they are. My research (Whitehead, 2003) has identified a number of factors that help deeper learning to take place and that can encourage people to engage with what they are reflecting on, thinking about, experiencing and learning at a deeper level. These will be helpful to consider when you are planning to facilitate learning and/or reflection.

Connectedness to experience

Deep learning and reflection will be experiential at various levels. It will be an experience in and of itself, and may encourage participants to try new things or engage in new experiences. It will also draw on and take account of previous knowledge and experience as part of the process, and assist in helping people connect their learning and reflection with their present and future experience. Often the mutual sharing of experiences within the group is as helpful as receiving facilitator input. As a facilitator, this is a way of sharing power with the group and emphasizing the co-intentional nature of learning and reflection. When you have in a group people with experience that is complementary to and perhaps greater than yours, it is also a great way of drawing on this rather than feeling threatened or intimidated by it.

Purposefulness

Effective learning and reflection will feel purposeful to those taking part. In this regard the purpose and aims should be clear and explicit throughout, to help people have a greater sense of ownership and engagement.

Variety

A varied approach maximizes the potential for effective engagement, can increase enjoyment, combat boredom and should help to complement participants' different learning styles by providing a selection of ways into material. I see this as a kind of 'layering' process as we give opportunity for learning to be approached, explored and integrated in different ways. Variety can also be brought into a session through including variations in levels of participants' involvement, the pace of the session, different kinds of activity, levels of emotional intensity and personal disclosure. It is important that variety is purposeful and well thought through, so that it contributes to the overall learning or reflection journey. If you are struggling to think of different ways of working, the 52 suggestions in Table 1 may be helpful.

Environment

This area is covered in Chapter 3, so I don't intend to comment further here, except to underline its importance once again!

Table 1 Approaches to learning and reflection

Analysing a picture	Hot seating	Memory exercise	Sharing experience
Blob trees	Ice-breaker game	Preparing a presentation	Simulation game
Card sorting exercise	Interviewing an individual	Problem page	Skills inventory Still pictures
Case study	Life-maps	Problem-solving	Symbols and metaphors
Creating drama sketches	Listening in pairs exercise	Questionnaire	Taking photographs
Debate	Listening to a story	Quiz	Thought shower/ idea blitz
Demonstration	Listening to a talk or sermon	Reading	Top-ten rating/ organizing
Designing coat of arms	Listening to music/song	Reflecting on a poem	Treasure hunt
Discussion	Making a CD/DVD	Reflection using postcards	Trip or visit
Fishbowl	Making a collage	Role play	Visual diagram or chart
Group or individual mind map	Making vox pops	Scavenger hunt	Watching a film clip
Guided reflection	Matching exercise	Self-assessment	Working out puzzles
Handout/ worksheet	Meditation		World Café

Congruence

Congruence is about how things flow together. If there is a mismatch between the content of what is being looked at and the facilitator's attitude, words or behaviour, the process will feel discordant, a little like the scratching of fingernails across a blackboard! There needs to be congruence too between the content and the methods and approaches used. Where possible, seek to model what you are talking about through your methodology. Integration of facilitator attitude, behaviour, content, methodology and process is likely to increase the levels of integration experienced by participants, even if they are unaware of it.

Multisensory approaches

> We need a *pedagogy of the senses* . . . Our senses need to be taught. They are gateways, thresholds between us and the world around; but also between soul and body. They form a bridge, just as imagination is a bridge between notional and concrete reality. And they are the means by which relationship is established.   (Creaven, 2003:79)

This image of a bridge is helpful with regard to deep learning. Although the effective use of the senses has been well documented in regard to early-years learning, it is something I have found incredibly useful in working with people of all ages in ministry contexts. Chapter 5 highlights some key principles around using multisensory approaches, and I believe they are particularly valuable when it comes to facilitating learning and reflection.

Group factors

Group factors can contribute hugely to people's ability to learn and reflect. Dysfunctional group relationships and dynamics can distract and can undermine people's experience. If they are to learn or reflect effectively, they need to be able to engage with the processes of what is going on rather than being preoccupied by the dynamics of the group, by dominant individuals or by anxiety (whether conscious or unconscious).

How people learn and reflect

Over the past few years there has been significant debate about the helpfulness or otherwise of learning-styles theory. The different models are inevitably flawed and risk over-simplification. The reality is that we are complex individuals whose learning preferences are affected by many different factors, including personality type, context, prior educational experience, motivation levels, perceptions, mood and relationships. These challenges notwithstanding, I believe learning-theory can provide a helpful starting point in designing learning processes for individuals and groups.

Four learning styles

Honey and Mumford (1992) have identified four preferred learning styles. These are summarized here, with some suggestions for the kinds of learning activities that would work effectively with each.

Activists

Activist learners tend to enjoy learning by doing. They engage enthusiastically with hands-on learning and will often be the first to participate in an exercise or activity. They often contribute to discussions immediately, without taking time to think things through. They enjoy challenges, appear enthusiastic and like variety in learning. Routine and repetition can bore them and they tend not to be keen on sitting and listening for long periods. Activists tend to enjoy discussion, small groups, simulation or management games, craft activities like drawing or modelling, role play, trips and practical projects.

Reflectors

Reflective learners tend to think carefully about what they are learning and like to have enough time to think things through or research. They can sometimes appear quiet in a group, and because they take time to think, can sometimes appear to take a back seat or lack interest in discussions. They will often contribute the most insightful and perceptive questions or comments once they have had time to think. They enjoy hearing and considering different perspectives, appreciate clear instructions and boundaries, like to understand what is expected, and don't like to be pushed for answers or to be made the centre of attention. They can become frustrated when a session appears to be rushed or things are skipped over. They tend to enjoy discussions, debates, question-and-answer sessions, researching, quiet space to think as part of a session, talks, video, film and one-to-one work.

Theorists

Theorists tend to enjoy understanding how things fit together. They often work by making connections and finding patterns, and learn best when they can see the way learning fits into a whole picture. They enjoy logical approaches, questioning and exploring issues. They will often ask deep questions and like to be stretched in their thinking, enjoying the freedom to play with ideas but often putting these into clear patterns or frameworks. They can become frustrated with woolly or 'touchy-feely' activities and things that are not explained sufficiently or backed up rationally. They dislike ideas and approaches that appear contradictory. They tend to enjoy debate, discussion, models and diagrams showing how things fit together, analysis, talks and lectures.

Pragmatists

Pragmatic learners like to relate learning to life and learn best when the learning is clearly relevant. They often ask practical questions, enthusiastically link learning to practice and will earth ideas in the everyday. They enjoy practical, skills-based activities and relevant, down-to-earth discussion. They like new ideas that can be practically tested but don't enjoy situations that feel irrelevant or discussions that focus on ideas rather than practicalities. Pragmatists tend to enjoy practical projects, case studies, role plays, real-life simulation games, demonstrations and problem-solving.

Spiritual pathways

Another way of considering approaches to learning and reflection, particularly in a more devotional context, is to draw on an understanding of different 'spiritual pathways' (Ortberg and Barton, 2001). This model considers how individuals connect and relate to God.

- Those with a **relational** preference find it easiest to connect to God through relationship with others, through strong relationships with other Christians, belonging to small groups and corporate prayer or Bible Study.
- Those with an **intellectual** preference connect to God through learning and tend to be thinkers who enjoy Bible study and theology, problem-solving, reading and listening to good preaching and teaching.
- Those with a preference for **serving** connect to God through helping others, having a specific role and learning as they serve. They

can be supported to see God at work in their places of serving and by soaking their serving in prayer.

- Those with a **worship** preference connect most effectively to God through praise and worship. In a session they are likely to find it helpful to have opportunity to engage in corporate worship or have worship music playing in the background during times of reflection.

- People with an **activist** preference have a strong sense of vision and a passion to work for God and develop the potential in others. They will enjoy learning and reflection that is more task focused and will relish being stretched and challenged. They may find it helpful to be encouraged to use journalling or other active approaches to reflection to help them focus.

- Those who are **contemplative** enjoy connecting to God through time alone and will relish space within gatherings for opportunity to pray and spend time in solitude. Space is important.

- Those with a **creation** preference connect best to God through experiencing creation and nature and are refreshed and renewed through being out of doors. They will often find multisensory and visual approaches helpful.

Using preferences in planning

Understanding the different ways in which people learn and connect can be useful in helping us to plan processes to work with individuals or groups. For many people, the default approach will be either to work to their own preferred style or copy models adopted by their organizational culture or by those who have influenced them. Understanding and working with a range of different styles will help you engage with learners who might have a different style from yours, and will hopefully mean that all individuals in a group are able to engage with what is going on in a way that works for them.

In practice it is helpful to recognize that designing processes that engage with all of the four learning styles above will assist us in ensuring that we go right through the learning cycle (Whitehead, 2003). Some activities can be designed to engage with a range of styles and preferences, and seeking to plan sessions or gatherings that meet the needs of different learners will encourage us to bring variety, pace and layering into our processes (see Figure 13, overleaf).

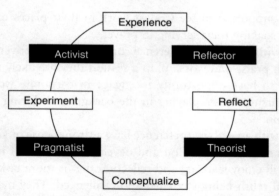

Figure 13 Learning styles and the learning cycle

For action and reflection

- Think about experiences of learning and reflection that have been facilitated by others. What have you found helpful? What has not been helpful?
- How would you describe your own learning style or preferred approaches? How do these influence the ways you facilitate learning or reflection for others?
- Look through the approaches to learning and reflection in Table 1 (p. 121). Which do you think work with which learning preference? Which of these could you use or adopt that you have never used before?
- To what extent does the learning or reflection you undertake encourage deep learning? How could you use some of the suggestions in this chapter to develop your practice to see this happen more?

11

Facilitating decision-making processes

SALLY NASH

> King Arthur wanted a lot more than a Camelot of dreams,
> soaring out of the morning mist . . . He wanted a smart
> Camelot, a collective enterprise that functioned intelligently.
> (David Perkins)

Many of us might share King Arthur's dream and hope, metaphorically at least, for a round table of dynamic, engaged decision-makers.
However, there is often significant work to be done for this dream to
become reality. Perkins suggests that left to themselves, conversations
in organizations 'commonly gravitate towards counterproductive
patterns of autocracy, secrecy, rivalry, narrowness, confusion, and
more' (2003:14). If collective decision-making is to be effective, there
needs to be a better way.

Adopting a facilitative approach to decision-making is likely to
appeal more to those who have an open, approachable, democratic
style of leadership, as inevitably sharing decision-making will result
in potential loss of control and there is some risk inherent in sharing
power. Not everyone will fundamentally agree with leading in this
way. Sid wrote a paper for his church leader proposing changing to
a structure based around genuine participation and sharing of power.
His church leader was horrified and explained that they would
lose all their power if such a thing happened. Sadly this is not a rare
occurrence. Pimlott (2009:8) suggests there are five reasons why a
more participative approach to decision-making is important:

1 it produces better outcomes (the efficiency argument);
2 it enhances and develops the ability and capacity of individuals to
   take responsibility and bring about change in their own contexts
   and lives (the empowerment argument);
3 it is the morally right and just way to work (the equity argument);

4 it is a higher humane calling (the philosophical argument);
5 it is a theological imperative (the divine argument).

This last argument is based on an understanding of the Trinity as a participative, empowering community (Fiddes, 2000), which the church can help to reflect. This chapter will explore different approaches to facilitating decision-making and how this can be done more effectively.

Preparation

Good preparation is vital in facilitating decision-making and can help with the management of expectations, which otherwise can derail decision-making. An effective facilitator should think through what needs to be done before any meeting or process is initiated. Group decision-making can be complex, with a range of factors to consider: all the relevant information is not necessarily accessible; there are often a range of alternative decisions that can be made, each of which has different implications; and the reaction of people to decisions made is sometimes unpredictable and may need careful management.

Perhaps the most crucial issue in facilitating decision-making processes is identifying what level of participation and empowerment is going to be involved in the process. The range of possibilities include:

- the group has the authority to make the decision itself;
- the group is responsible for both the decision and the implementation;
- the group is being asked for an opinion or recommendation that will go to another group for a final decision;
- an individual is responsible for making a decision but is using a group to help in the process;
- a range of options are being explored and the pros and cons of each are being discussed as part of an ongoing decision-making process.

Frustration ensues when groups are not clear about the scope and authority of a meeting or process, so setting this out at the beginning is vital. If you are a facilitator without the capacity to determine the scope of the decision-making, ensure you are clear about your mandate for a meeting so that expectations can be fulfilled on all sides.

The next thing to decide is what approach or methodology is best suited to your particular context. Some church structures will have decision-making processes written into their governance that will apply in specified situations, but there will be many other situations where a process will need to be identified and adopted. Again, it is important to ensure that the group is aware of the format and content of the meeting, and in some contexts an advance briefing may be useful, particularly when people need time to think through particular issues, research, prepare arguments, pray or reflect on their own viewpoints. Mind Tools – <www.mindtools.com> – suggests that there are six steps to be followed in effective decision-making:

1 create a constructive environment;
2 generate good alternatives;
3 explore these alternatives;
4 choose the best alternative;
5 check your decision;
6 communicate your decision, and take action.

This provides a very simple outline for a facilitator to follow, although there are a variety of approaches and techniques that may be helpful in accomplishing this.

In many contexts where you are facilitating decision-making there will be an element of change involved. David Cormack (1995:37) has developed a list of the sort of attitudes that may be found in any group, which it can be helpful to consider when approaching group decision-making (see Table 2, overleaf).

Beginning the process

At the beginning of the decision-making process there are a range of things it may be helpful to establish. This includes the scope of the decision and the approach to be used, discussed above. It will normally be important to establish ground rules (see pages 42–3). Edmondson (2010:84) offers some ground rules based on the African Indaba process that might be helpful with groups who are not used to setting ground rules:

Table 2 Group attitudes to decision-making

Type description	Typical attitudes
Radical	Loves to pioneer new initiatives. All change is wonderful and exciting. Nothing is good around here. Everything has to change and has to change fast and I'm the one to do it! Traditionalists are reactionaries.
Progressive	Likes the pioneer but prefers a slower rate of change. Most change is exciting as long as there is not too much risk. Not everything needs to change, but most does.
Conservative	Suspicious of the radical pioneer. Most change is somewhat threatening. Most things are OK around here. A little fine-tuning here and there never did anyone any harm.
Traditional	Radicals are revolutionaries and hence very dangerous. All change is very threatening. Things are OK here apart from what has been changed recently. Let us go back to the good old days.
Progressive Conservative or Conservative Progressive	Change is necessary, but people view change differently. Traditionalists need to be encouraged to change. Radicals need to be taught caution. All change is not necessarily good; people are good.

- Listen sincerely and speak with integrity.
- It is acceptable to disagree but this runs alongside a commitment to maintain relationship and respect of others' viewpoints.
- It is important to speak in the first person.
- This process is not about 'win–lose'.
- We must each ask ourselves the question: 'What sacrifices am I prepared to make and what generous initiatives might I take, in order to move things forward?

Another area to consider addressing is a possible feeling that consensus should be the norm in a Christian context, but this is not always possible and thus alternatives need to be explored. Introducing Stephen Covey's fourth habit of 'highly effective people', 'win–win', can be relevant, particularly where a decision might be contentious. It is based on the idea that we are socialized into seeing our self-worth in relation to others; we focus on competition and comparison and think that resources are limited and we need to fight for our share. However, win–win is about co-operation and collaboration, not competition, and is an attitude that can be adopted by everyone. Covey (undated) suggests that to adopt this win–win attitude there are three characteristics we should have:

- integrity – sticking with your true feelings, values, and commitments;
- maturity – expressing your ideas and feelings with courage and consideration for the ideas and feelings of others;
- abundance mentality – believing there is plenty for everyone.

Introducing such concepts can be useful ways of reminding people how we should relate to one another.

You may also want to talk about what your understanding is of the role of the facilitator in this context or what your role is within the church or organization if this is not known by all. For example, talking about her contribution to a group, Widdicombe offers some ideas that could form part of an introduction to a session:

> I may have valuable insights and useful ideas to contribute to a decision making process or to an individual or a group, but I do not have all the answers. In relation to groups, I believe in maximising the combined resources, the wealth of experience, ideas and insights of all the members in order to reach wise conclusions and achieve decisions which have everyone's backing. (1994:37)

To start off a process or generate some ideas there are a variety of exercises that can be used. Two simple ones that act as an ice-breaker – or can be used to generate comments later in the process – are snowballs and paper planes, which have the advantage of a degree of anonymity. With snowballs, everyone is given a piece of paper; they then write their question or response on it, screw it into a ball and try to throw it into a bucket or similar. The snowballs are then distributed and people read out the responses or questions. With paper planes, people write down their response to the facilitator's question then make a paper plane and fly it across the room. Then someone else comments on the first comment. This could go on five or six times. A similar exercise can be carried out by simply passing pieces of paper round a circle.

Getting into the process

As a facilitator, it is essential to be able to identify the helpful and less helpful contributions, both from your perspective and the participants'. Perkins (2003) suggests that generative contributions include clarifying, probing, testing, openness and constructing, and degenerative ones include dismissing, asserting, defensiveness, negative critique and isolating. As a facilitator, it is particularly important to model good practice and find ways to affirm people while gently challenging, where appropriate, the less helpful contributions. Perkins uses the terms 'needs' and 'moves' to describe what is required for good collective decision-making. Needs include: information; multiple perspectives (which means carefully thinking through who should be part of the decision-making process); being able to deal with complexity because of a potentially vast range of possibilities and consequences; and being able to deal with negative emotions. Moves include: identifying options, including the less obvious ones; looking at what both the short-term and long-term consequences are of the best options; and evaluating them in the light of the significant factors before coming to a resolution that takes into account priorities.

Potential problems

There is a children's game called 'stuck in the mud' where if touched by 'it' you have to stand still until someone comes and releases you so you can get back into the game. It can be enormously frustrating waiting to be released! As a facilitator, there will be times when you need to have strategies to release groups from stuckness. Groups get stuck in different ways: sometimes through distraction and going off on side tracks not pertinent to the topic, or going round in circles; other times because of power plays, which includes a few dominating discussions inhibiting others or factions or cliques that are resistant to working together. Such potential problems are not necessarily recognized by everyone in the group, but it can lessen energy and commitment and cause frustration. A variety of strategies can help when groups are facing these problems:

- revisiting (or establishing) ground rules and reminding the group how they have agreed to work together;
- giving a period of silence for people to reflect and process their thoughts;
- breaking the group down into twos or threes to talk about the issues and report back, which enables less vocal members to get their views heard;

- specifically asking if anyone wants to add something or has a different perspective, or if anyone who has not spoken has something to share;
- considering whether some mapping of where you are up to or taking a vote to establish people's views might help clarify things;
- taking particular care to be affirming of all contributions and to encourage careful and attentive listening;
- reflecting on whether you need to amend your facilitation style in the light of people's responses;
- addressing the unhelpful behaviour of individuals;
- contemplating naming some of the issues that are being experienced, particularly if there is an elephant in the room.

If a group is particularly challenging, you may want to consider co-facilitation, which gives you someone else to compare notes with; and ideally, if it is someone with complementary skills and personality, you may each be able to mitigate different problems.

Sometimes when facilitating decision-making processes the emotions of participants can cause difficulties. It may be important to help people name and engage with the emotions they are experiencing. There may be times when it is worth considering which emotions may be particularly triggered by the topic and asking people: 'How are you feeling at this stage?' Then perhaps add some potential feelings – sometimes people don't recognize what it is they are feeling until someone else names it. Potential negative emotions may include frustration, anger, hurt, disappointment, fear, sadness, shame; potential positive emotions may include joy, relief, excitement, anticipation, delight, elation, peace.

World Café – an approach to facilitating bigger groups

One of the approaches that can be used to facilitate participation, and one that is more informal than many traditional church or organization meetings, is the World Café (Brown and Isaacs, 2005). You need to name the café to correspond with what you hope to accomplish, so it is clear what the purpose is – for example, Developing Small Group Café, Baptism Café, Community Café, Spiritual Practices Café. Basically the room is set out in café style, with paper table-covers, pens, refreshments and someone designated as a conversation host on each table. The individual or, more usually, team organizing the event would have a series of questions that are discussed at the tables; the conversation host facilitates the discussion. This role of conversation host is key and the scope of it is encapsulated thus:

> As a conversation host, ask yourself: What can I do to make whomever I'm with feel physically comfortable, emotionally safe, and intellectually challenged? How can I support members in discovering a deeper understanding and appreciation – for each other and for the questions we're exploring? How can I engage the Café participants themselves in hosting each other and in discovering the magic in the middle of their conversations. (Brown and Isaacs, 2005:161)

The people taking on this role need to be carefully chosen and well prepared and briefed.

The World Café has seven key principles that work together in achieving the purpose.

1 Set the context – clarify the purpose and broad parameters within which the dialogue will unfold.
2 Create hospitable space – assure the welcoming environment and psychological safety that nurtures personal comfort and mutual respect.
3 Explore questions that matter – focus collective attention on powerful questions that attract collaborative engagement.
4 Encourage everyone's contribution – enliven the relationship between the 'me' and the 'we' by inviting full participation and mutual giving.
5 Cross-pollinate and connect diverse perspectives – create a sense of dynamic interaction through engaging with a range of diverse perspectives while retaining a common focus on core questions.
6 Listen together for patterns, insights and deeper questions – focus shared attention in ways that nurture coherence of thought without losing individual contribution.
7 Harvest and share collective discoveries – make collective knowledge and insight visible and actionable (Brown and Isaacs, 2005:174).

One of the interesting things about the World Café methodology is that it sees the approach to the individual as encouraging and honouring the uniqueness of contributions as more effective as a focus than empowerment or participation. If you think this is a potentially helpful approach, there are plenty of free resources available from <www.theworldcafe.com>, including questions that could be useful, whichever methodology you are using. Some of the most generally helpful among those are (Brown and Isaacs, 2005:173):

- What question, if answered, could make the greatest difference to the future of the situation we are exploring here?
- What's important to you about this situation and why do you care?
- What do we know so far/still need to learn about the situation?
- What have you heard that had real meaning for you? What surprised you? What puzzled or challenged you? What question would you like to ask now?
- How can we support each other in taking the next steps? What unique contribution can we each make?
- What conversation, if begun today, could ripple out in a way that created new possibilities for the future?

Evaluating decisions

While it is helpful to have established the criteria for making a decision at the beginning of the process, it is important to revisit this as you approach the final decision. There is a wide range of ways of doing this, and the Mind Tools website has 40 or so – <www.mindtools.com>. With complex, serious or particularly important decisions it may be useful to engage in a discernment process.

An Ignatian approach

A very simple process drawn from Ignatian spirituality would involve asking people to imagine implementing the decision and considering how it feels, and then imagining not implementing the decision and seeing how that feels. Preceding this you would usually pray for the Holy Spirit to guide people in this time and for the feelings associated with the exercise to emerge from a process focused on trusting the work of the Holy Spirit in people. A fuller version of this is offered by Widdicombe (1994):

Step 1　Seek reasons for going a particular way and ask everyone to meditate on their own about this and write down their response. All then share what they have written, listening closely to each other (if the group is very big this can be done in smaller groups). Participants then reflect again on what they have heard.

Step 2 Seek reasons against going in this way and then repeat the three steps above.

Step 3 Weigh the reasons for and against using the processes above.

Heart, hand, mind

Another approach to evaluating options or decisions is to use the formula heart, hand, mind:

- *Heart* – what makes it emotionally engaging?
- *Hand* – what makes it tangible and practical?
- *Mind* – what makes it logical and sensible?

Having listed responses to each of these questions, they can then be marked from 1 to 10, the strengths and weaknesses evaluated and a decision made (Gray, Brown and Macanufo, 2010:179).

Dot votes

Dot votes can be helpful in evaluating options or decisions. Each person is given, say, five dots – stickers work well – and is asked to distribute these across the various options, ranging from giving all five to one or one to each of five.

After-action review

Perkins (2003:53) commends a US Army tool, the after-action review (AAR), which asks four questions:

- What was the intent?
- What actually happened?
- What have we learnt?
- What do we do now?

This can be a useful simple formula to evaluate the decision-making processes and learn for future occasions.

Conclusion

Facilitating decision-making processes can be one of the greatest challenges in ministry, particularly when the decision is significant and much is invested by many in the situation. The majority of decisions will involve change, and change can be both threatening and inspiring. David Cormack's prayer for change provides comfort and hope and the realization that we don't have to make decisions alone:

> Wisdom and Love, you call us to share in the rebirth of your creation. Through Christ the possibilities of change become limitless and the power to change is made available to me. In Christ's power may I affirm the message of change in this world, nurture your people oppressed for change's sake, discover Christ at work in dark places of this world, receive the forgiveness that frees me from my fear of change, embrace those from whom I am tempted to turn away because I think they cannot be changed, witness to the truth that you are the God of all change, and welcome all I meet as pilgrims on the road of change. So may I be ready for all the changes you give. And may I be drawn more deeply into the transforming fellowship of your Holy Spirit. Through Jesus Christ our Lord. Amen. (1995:207)

For action and reflection

- Which of the reasons for adopting participatory approaches to decision-making are most important for you?
- What attitudes to change are most difficult for you to deal with? How does your own attitude influence your facilitation?
- Think of an occasion when the group you were facilitating got stuck. What did you do? What else might you have done?
- Is there an area of ministry where a World Café event may be useful?

12

Facilitating change

SIMON SUTCLIFFE

See, I am doing a new thing! Now it springs up; do you not perceive it? I am making a way in the wilderness and streams in the wasteland. (Isaiah 43.19)

Any chapter dealing with facilitating change is a mammoth task as change and transformation happen at personal, micro and macro levels (Cameron and Green, 2012). Change at the personal level concerns formation, growth and character. It is part of the ongoing journey of being human and takes on particular significance concerning Christian discipleship. Macro-level change has to do with massive institutions and nations. It is the process of becoming more efficient, better organized and the result is 'success' (however you might want to term that: economic growth, reduced waiting lists, higher results and so on).

Micro-level change sits in between personal and macro and is the main focus of this chapter, which explores facilitating change at a local level, within a congregation or group. This could encompass anything from a change of leadership to having new carpets in the meeting room. I will be using the theme of missional change within congregations to explore the issues, challenges and processes around change, but the key principles can be applied and contextualized to assist in facilitating change in a wide range of different situations and locations.

Missional change

'Missional' is a word often used in fresh expression and emerging church circles but rarely defined. At Fresh Expressions conferences people speak of 'being missional' or of 'missional communities', and most will understand what is hinted at. I want to suggest that the word has three definite facets:

1 Its focus is on those at the edges of or beyond the Christian community. (Gibbs and Bolger, 2006:51ff.)
2 Its activities resonate with what the Church understands as Kingdom. (McLaren, 2010:196ff.)
3 It requires imagination and courage. (Frost and Hirsch, 2011:27ff.)

These facets are not limited to the church-planting movements and can be equally helpful to the inherited church. Parish, church or congregational renewal, then, is the inherited church focusing its attention on those who are on the edges or beyond its current activities, is deeply rooted in an understanding of Kingdom and will demand a spirit of creativity and commitment.

Enabling a church to be more missional is the focus of this chapter – at the forefront are questions of how this change process might be facilitated and what is required of the facilitator.

Penguins and icebergs

A quick internet search for management techniques will provide enough material to absorb the rest of your ministry. Most of it belongs to the world of business, industry and commerce and, I believe, is not always easily transferable to church leadership (Cameron and Green, 2012; Green, 2007; Bridges, 2009). However, one book I have found useful over the years is Kotter's and Rathgeber's *Our Iceberg is Melting* (2006). It might be criticized for its lack of sophistication but I have found it very helpful when trying to facilitate change in the context of ministry in a local church. The book is about a penguin named Fred who recognizes that the iceberg that the penguins live on is melting and that sometime in the future it will not be able to sustain the penguin colony. The story outlines the process by which the penguins can move to another iceberg, but to do so they have to overcome tradition, resistance and scepticism.

This story helps the authors outline their eight-stage process for managing change:

1 create a sense of urgency;
2 form a guiding team;
3 develop the change vision and strategy;
4 communicate the vision;
5 empower others to act;

6 create short-term wins;
7 build on the change;
8 create a new culture.

I use this not as a model that we must stick to slavishly but as a platform to think more concretely about the process of facilitating change in congregations. The boundaries between each step are not as distinct as the model might at first suggest. It is very likely that the urgency and vision will be shaped and reshaped throughout the process and that obstacles will need to be removed the whole time.

Urgency: identifying the problem

Part of the problem for facilitators is recognizing the need for change. Within the church that need comes from a number of sources. First, it could be argued that *being missional* is core to the DNA of the church (Frost and Hirsch, 2003:23ff.). A New Testament lecturer once told me that 'the early church grew because it never occurred to it not to'. It could be argued that if there is no identifiable way in which a congregation is impacting on its locality then something different needs to happen. Another way in which the urgency might present itself is through identified need. At the time of writing, a mass of food-banks working with the Trussell Trust – <www.trusselltrust.org> – are emerging around the country, responding to the needs of local communities as churches become more aware of the plight of those who go hungry.

There are also times when problems are the catalyst and present facilitators with the opportunity to enable a much larger vision to emerge. For instance, a church is flooded out, which causes a great deal of damage and will require refurbishment. Simultaneously a local charity has been forced to leave its office because the rent is too high, and there has been a constant grumbling in the church that a greater variety of worship styles could be used were the church worship area not so small. All these troubles come together and the facilitator can begin to perceive how a solution to all three problems might be found in a bold renovation plan.

The facilitator must be aware, at this early stage, not to move from facilitation into manipulation. If the case is overstated or is simply the desire of the facilitator, it can easily become a tool to control or manipulate. One way to avoid this is to ensure that urgency is grounded into contextual reality. This can be done through observation, raw data and anecdotal evidence. For example, you receive a phone call one evening telling you that some young people are on top of the church building (observation). You go with a colleague to the church and ask the young people to get down. You explain to them that you are worried about their safety and possible damage to the building; they tell you they have nowhere else to go since the old recreation ground was shut down (anecdotal). Over the coming weeks you notice young people standing in bus stops and outside local shops (observation) and you wonder if this has always been the case or if you have only started to notice it after the church roof incident. The next time you are in the shop you ask the shopkeeper if she has noticed any difference. She explains that she has and that even though the young people aren't doing anything illegal they do put elderly people off coming into the shop (anecdotal). You decide to go home and check on the internet for local statistics that confirm that the population of young people in the area is steadily rising and that there are no facilities for them in the neighbourhood (raw data/ statistical).

In this situation the urgency to be involved in youth work comes not because the church wants to have its congregation full of young people – although that might be a wonderful by-product – but because the church has recognized a need that is supported by what has been observed and spoken about, and the available research data of others. In sharing this need with the wider church the facilitator can present this information with the question: 'What do we do about it?' The answer might be to employ a youth worker, but it might be to lobby the local council robustly to provide resources for young people in the area. Whatever course of action is taken, it will benefit greatly from rigorous research that will inform and potentially help ease the change process.

Change: a corporate responsibility

The business of change demands the need for discernment, and discernment is best achieved through conferring (see, for example, Shier-Jones, 2005:47). Gathering a group of people in prayer to discover where the Holy Spirit is prompting is embedded deep in Christian tradition. If facilitators try to bring about change on their own it ceases to be facilitation and becomes management (at best) or dictatorship (at worst). One of the first tasks of the facilitator, therefore, is to gather a group of people who can formulate a vision and a future plan. Much of the facilitator's work then centres around ensuring the group operates effectively and achieves its aims.

John Kotter identifies the different characters you need in order to form a successful team – <www.kotterinternational.com>. This is clearly an advantage in industry but is much more difficult for the Church, where facilitators generally have a much smaller pool of people to work with and limited resources. Some of the key team roles have been explored and identified in Chapter 4, but it is helpful to consider those who are particularly useful to have around when it comes to facilitating change.

- *Permission givers* – those who have authority to make important decisions. You don't need all the permission givers to be part of the group responsible for outlining, sharing and implementing the vision, but it is helpful to have some of them.
- *Administrators* – those who will see that letters are written and spreadsheets completed. They are also often completer-finishers and so will usually ensure the job is seen through to a successful conclusion.
- *People of influence* – those who have the respect of others and are trusted.
- *Dreamers* – those who are imaginative and creative and can see beyond the present reality into new and exciting possibilities.
- *Workers* – those who will get jobs done: set out chairs, organize food, do the washing up and so on. Often this is the least glamorous role, but the group cannot function properly without them.
- *Theologians* – those who can interpret the vision and locate it in the story of the Church. Theologians are often overlooked but they are essential if the Church is to be more than a statutory agency. If the facilitator is the vicar/minister/pastor, he or she is often the most theologically literate person in the group, to whom this role should default.
- *Facilitator* – the role of the facilitator is to have an overall view of the group and the work it needs to carry out. The facilitator needs to be particularly attentive to vision and process – outlined

below – and might need to remind the group of them regularly. He or she will be concerned for transparency, honesty and integrity so that all those affected by the change will know what information is available and how to access it. It could be possible, if it is not already assumed, that the facilitator will carry some pastoral responsibility.

It might be that one person holds more than one of these characteristics, but more than two or three would be unlikely. Therefore it is essential that a large enough team be brought together to enable effective functioning, but not so many that members disable each other. More often than not a church cannot find enough people to make up an effective team, and facilitators may need to look for people with the right qualities outside the congregation. They might come from other local groups who are sympathetic to the vision (ecumenical colleagues, the twinning association, parish council . . .) or might work for a statutory agency (local health workers, the youth service, police . . .).

Encouraging change: key questions

The four middle steps of Kotter's and Rathgeber's process are, for me, the business of bringing about change. This begins with developing a plan or vision of how the future might look differently. The Judaeo-Christian narrative is rich with stories of hope about a different future. From the exilic prophecies in Isaiah to Paul's hope of the imminent return of Christ, we can see that a different future shapes the inheritance of the Church. The group's task is to begin to imagine what an alternative future might look like – for the church building, the young people, the hungry in the city and so on – and then develop a plan where that vision might become a reality. *The key questions for the group to ask at this stage are: 'Who will be blessed?' and 'How do we participate in that blessing?'*

Once a vision and plan have been formulated, the next task is to communicate them to the wider church. This is a very sensitive part of the process of bringing about change. As with discerning the need, the facilitator must be wary of manipulation. *The key questions at this stage are: 'Who are the stakeholders?' and 'How do they normally communicate?'* Stakeholders are people and groups who will be directly affected by the vision proposed. The impact is likely to affect the whole church but might have a particular impact on certain groups – the ladies' fellowship, the choir and so on. It might also affect those outside the church, such as church user groups or the specific group of people the church is hoping to bless.

When the stakeholders have been identified, the group must decide how best to communicate the vision to them, being honest about any impact it will have on them and any expectations placed upon them. Not all groups will respond positively to a PowerPoint presentation in the church meeting room. Some, especially permission givers, might want to see a written report that details the contextual findings, the vision, the plan to meet that vision and the financial and legal implications. Another group might prefer to have a conversation in their group setting. There might be a need to visit people in their homes, and the power of blogs and social media cannot be underestimated in twenty-first-century communication. What is important is that the form of communication be suited to the people being communicated to. This means that one vision might have to have a variety of ways of being heard and, more importantly, understood.

Once the vision has been cast and others have been caught up in and excited about it, then the hard work begins of seeing this vision become a reality. The facilitator's role now extends beyond the initial group and moves out to other members of the congregation, who will look for permission to be involved and may need to be empowered to utilize their gifts as the plan takes shape. People are more likely to be involved if they can see identifiable roles or jobs that need to be done. This might mean instilling confidence in others and may involve quietly putting right things that have not gone to plan.

This is also the time when specialist help might be required, such as the Trussell Trust for a foodbank or an architect and builder for a church renovation. *The key questions to ask are: 'What specialisms do we need?', 'What are the lines of accountability?' and 'What are the reporting requirements?'*

It helps, especially if implementing the vision will take some time, to have moments that can be used as markers that the vision is progressing, and in the right direction. This aids momentum and offers encouragement to those involved. These moments ought to carry with them a sense of celebration – for example, a party for the laying of the first stone, or an act of worship on the place where a new play park is to be built. *The question to ask here is: 'How do we celebrate in this community?'*

The place of resistance

Up to now we have assumed a smooth process of change with little or no resistance. Most people in church leadership know this is highly unlikely. Resistance, however, is not always the same and not always destructive (Hobgood, 2001). Resistance in the form of challenging questions is useful, even if uncomfortable, as it forces the facilitator and group to hone their vision and work out the detail of implementation. Sometimes resistance is born out of memory. I was once warned by someone on my church leadership team about the impossibility of an ecumenical harvest festival for the village. I was surprised by this, especially as the church leaders were very much in favour. When it did not go ahead because other church leadership teams did not want it, I went to see the individual concerned and asked about the background to her comment. She told me of the history of the robed choir in one church and that now the harvest festival was one of the few times they were able to participate in worship. The next year we incorporated the choir into the vision for a joint harvest festival and it was very successful. If I had paid attention to the memory of someone who I thought was just being awkward, it might have happened a year earlier.

The most likely cause of resistance is usually a lack of understanding, which means that the group needs to work on articulating the vision and plan more effectively. If you can generate a passion and excitement about an alternative future, others will usually want to be involved. This might take longer than you had hoped but it is vital that others participate in seeing the vision come to fruition.

However, some resistance is difficult to overcome and is not positive. Often dissenters gather around other dissenters and form a coalition of resistance. Those dissenters might not be standing against the same thing: some might not like the new style of worship, some not look favourably on another group of people in the local community, but they gather together because they find some commonality in their dissension. The reality is that if this group is a majority, it is unlikely the change can happen at this time. If they are in a minority, the facilitator and the group need to decide whether they are going to forge ahead without them – a difficult decision that ought to be made prayerfully by the whole group.

It should be noted that if a vision for change is not seen through to completion, all is not lost – this chapter is written out of the wisdom of past failures! It does not mean the vision itself is wrong, but it might mean the time is not right or that there are lessons to learn about process. Both can be painful but they will enable the facilitator to be better prepared next time.

From project to change

Eventually the group needs to be disbanded and *life returns to normal*. This is can be a difficult time, especially for the group, who have invested so much in initiating and facilitating the change. But if the new thing is to be more than a project, it needs to become part of the culture of the church – whether new user groups are using a recently refurbished building, a congregation are enjoying a variety of worship styles, a youth programme is running in the village or the city's hungry are being fed. Eventually the alternative reality that was dreamed of in the first instance has to become the dominant reality for true change to have taken place. Putting an *end* to the project can be one of the *moments* to celebrate all that has been achieved, and reminds everyone involved that change is possible.

There are two consequences for the congregation. First, congregations that are used to change, however small, are more likely to adapt to change in the future. Some of the most daring and imaginative congregations I have worked with have been in rural areas where farmers, in a fast-changing agricultural economy, recognized the need for diversification long before the church did. Second, it brings us full circle to the opening statements about being missional, and in some small way the great prayer of the Church is realized – 'Thy Kingdom come'.

For action and reflection

- Make a list of the times you have been subject to change. It might be in a job reshuffle or as a member of the congregation. How did it feel? If it was a difficult experience, what could have helped to make it better? If it was a positive experience, what helped shape it?

- List the times you have facilitated change. Identify the high and low points of each process. What can you learn from these? How might this help you facilitate change in the future?
- What needs do you perceive in your community? How might you build a body of evidence to support your perception?
- What changes can you foresee for your local congregation in the next five years?
- When you look at the resources you have available for change, where are the gaps? Who might you need to work alongside?
- Who are the people most affected by the changes likely to happen in the foreseeable future? How might they participate in the change?

Bibliography

Adair, J. and Thomas, N. (eds) (2004), *The John Adair Handbook of Management and Leadership*, London: Thorogood.

Adirondack, S. (1998), *Just About Managing*, London: London Voluntary Service Council.

Baker, J. (2010), *Curating Worship*, London: SPCK.

Ballard, P. and Pritchard, J. (2006), *Practical Theology in Action: Christian Thinking in the Service of Church and Society*, 2nd edn, London: SPCK.

Beasley-Murray, P. (1998), *Power for God's Sake*, Carlisle: Paternoster.

Belbin, R. M. (1981), *Management Teams: Why they Succeed or Fail*, Oxford: Butterworth-Heinemann.

Belbin, R. M. (1993), *Team Roles at Work*, Oxford: Butterworth-Heinemann.

Berger, P. L. (1972), *An Invitation to Sociology*, Harmondsworth: Penguin.

Berger, P. L. and Luckmann, T. (1966), *The Social Construction of Reality: A Treatise in the Sociology of Knowledge*, Garden City, NY: Anchor Books.

Bion, W. (1961), *Experiences in Groups and Other Papers*, London: Tavistock Publications.

Bridges, W. (2009), *Managing Transitions*, 3rd edn, London: Nicholas Brearley.

Brockbank, A. and McGill, I. (1998), *Facilitating Reflective Learning in Higher Education*, Buckingham: Open University Press.

Brookfield, S. D. and Preskill, S. (1999), *Discussion as a Way of Teaching*, Buckingham: Open University Press.

Brown, J. and Isaacs, D. (2005), *The World Café*, San Francisco: Berrett-Koehler.

Brown, R. (1988), *Group Processes: Dynamics Within and Between Groups*, Oxford: Blackwell.

Buckingham, J. (1978), *Coping with Criticism*, South Plainfield, NJ: Bridge Publishing.

Buzan, T. (2010), *The Mind Map Book: Unlock Your Creativity, Boost Your Memory, Change Your Life*, Harlow: BBC Active.

Cameron, E. and Green, M. (2012), *Making Sense of Change Management*, London: Kogan Page.

Cameron, H., Richter, P., Davies, D. and Ward, F. (eds) (2005), *Studying Local Churches: A Handbook*, London: SCM Press.

Cormack, D. (1995), *Change Directions: New Ways Forward for Your Life, Your Church and Your Business*, Crowborough: Monarch.

Covey, S. (1989), *The Seven Habits of Highly Effective People*, London: Simon & Schuster.

Covey, S. R. (undated), 'Habit 4: Win Win', <www.stephencovey.com/7habits/7habits-habit4.php>, accessed 4 April 2012.

Creaven, F. (2003), *Body and Soul: A Spirituality of Imaginative Creativity*, London: SPCK.

Davis, M. (2002), *Walking on the Shore: A Way of Sharing Faith in Groups*, Chelmsford: Matthew James.

Earey, M. (2002), *Liturgical Worship: A Fresh Look, How it Works, Why it Matters*, London: Church House.

Edmondson, C. (2010), *Leaders Learning to Listen*, London: Darton, Longman & Todd.

Fiddes, P. S. (2000), *Participating in God: A Pastoral Doctrine of the Trinity*, Louisville, KY: Westminster John Knox.

Fleming Drane, O. M. (2002), *Clowns, Storytellers, Disciples: Spirituality and Creativity for Today's Church*, Oxford: Bible Reading Fellowship.

Freire, P. (1972), *Pedagogy of the Oppressed*, London: Penguin.

Frost, M. and Hirsch, A. (2003), *The Shaping of Things to Come: Innovation and Mission for the 21st-Century Church*, Peabody, MA: Hendrickson.

Frost, M. and Hirsch, A. (2011), *The Faith of Leap: Embracing a Theology of Risk, Adventure and Courage*, Grand Rapids, MI: Baker Books.

Gibbs, E. and Bolger, R. K. (2006), *Emerging Churches*, London: SPCK.

Gladwell, M. (2008), *Outliers*, London: Little Brown & Co.

Goleman, D. (1996), *Emotional Intelligence: Why it can Matter more than IQ*, London: Bloomsbury.

Gray, D., Brown, S. and Macanufo, J. (2010), *Gamestorming: A Playbook for Innovators, Rulebreakers, and Changemakers*, Sebastopol, CA: O'Reilly Media Inc.

Green, L. (1990), *Let's Do Theology: A Pastoral Cycle Resource Book*, London: Continuum.

Green, M. (2007), *Change Management Masterclass: A Step by Step Guide to Successful Change Management*, London: Kogan Page.

Hart, R. (1992), *Children's Participation from Tokenism to Citizenship*, Florence: UNICEF Innocenti Research Centre.

Hobgood, W. C. (2001), *Welcoming Resistance*, Bethesda, MD: The Alban Institute.

Hogan, C. (2003), *Practical Facilitation: A Toolkit of Techniques*, London: Kogan Page.

Honey, P. and Mumford, A. (1992), *The Manual of Learning Styles*, Maidenhead: Peter Honey.

Hunter, D., with Thorpe, S., Brown, H. and Bailey, A. (2007), *The Art of Facilitation: The Essentials for Leading Great Meetings and Creating Group Synergy*, rev. edn, San Francisco: Jossey-Bass.

Jaques, D. (1991), *Learning in Groups*, 2nd edn, London: Kogan Page.

Kahane, Adam (2004), *Solving Tough Problems: An Open Way of Talking, Listening, and Creating New Realities*, San Francisco: Berrett-Koehler.

Killen, P. O. and de Beer, J. (1994), *The Art of Theological Reflection*, New York: Crossroad.

Kline, N. (1999), *Time to Think*, London: Ward Lock.

Knowles, M. S., Holton, E. F. and Swanson, R. A. (1973), *The Adult Learner: The Definitive Classic in Adult Education and Human Resource Development*, 5th edn, Houston, TX: Gulf Publishing Co.

Kolb, David A. (1984), *Experiential Learning: Experience as the Source of Learning and Development*, Englewood Cliffs, NJ; London: Prentice Hall.

Kotter, J. and Rathgeber, H. (2006), *Our Iceberg is Melting: Changing and Succeeding Under Any Conditions*, London: Macmillan.

Lucas, J. (2006), 'Thirteen Things I Wished I'd Known about Preaching', in Haslam, G. (ed.), *Preach the Word!*, Lancaster: Sovereign World.

Macbeth, F. and Fine, N. (1995), *Playing with Fire: Creative Conflict Resolution for Young Adults*, Philadelphia, PA: New Society Publishers.

McLaren, B. D. (2010), *A New Kind of Christianity*, London: Hodder & Stoughton.

Male, D. (ed.) (2011), *Pioneers 4 Life: Explorations in Theology and Wisdom for Pioneering Leaders*, Abingdon: Bible Reading Fellowship.

Mallinson, J. (1996), *The Small Group Leader: A Manual to Develop Vital Small Groups*, Bletchley: Scripture Union.

Marshall, T. (1989), *Right Relationships: A Biblical Foundation for Making and Mending Relationships*, Chichester: Sovereign World Books.

Marton, F. and Säljö, R. (1976), 'On Qualitative Differences in Learning: I – Outcome and Process', *British Journal of Educational Psychology* 46:1, 4–11.

Nash, S., Pimlott, J. and Nash, P. (2008), *Skills for Collaborative Ministry*, London: SPCK.

National Advisory Committee on Creative and Cultural Education (NACCCE) (1999), *All Our Futures: Creativity, Culture and Education*, London: Department for Education and Employment.

Nouwen, H. J. (2007) [1972], *The Wounded Healer: Ministry in Contemporary Society*, London: Darton, Longman & Todd.

Ortberg, J. and Barton, R. H. (2001), *An Ordinary Day with Jesus: Experiencing the Reality of God in Your Everyday Life – Participant's Guide*, Barrington, IL: Willow Creek.

Palmer, P. J. (1983), *To Know as We are Known: A Spirituality of Education*, New York: Harper & Row.

Parsloe, E. and Wray, M. (2000), *Coaching and Mentoring*, London: Kogan Page.

Peberdy, D. and Hammersley, J. (2009), *Brilliant Meetings: What to Know, Do and Say to have Fewer, Better Meetings*, Harlow: Pearson Education.

Perkins, D. (2003), *King Arthur's Round Table: How Collaborative Conversations Create Smart Organizations*, Hoboken, NJ: Wiley.

Pimlott, N. (2009), 'Generating knowledge, exploring experience, improving practice: the use of group participative processes in Christian youth work', unpublished MA dissertation, Oxford Brookes University.

Potter, P. (2001), *The Challenge of Cell Church: Getting to Grips with Cell Church Values*, Oxford: Bible Reading Fellowship.

Ringer, T. M. (2002), *Group Action: The Dynamics of Groups in Therapeutic, Educational and Corporate Settings*, London: Jessica Kingsley.

Rogers, C. (1961), *On Becoming a Person*, Boston: Houghton Mifflin.

Runde, C. E. and Flanagan, T. A. (2008), *Building Conflict Competent Teams*, San Francisco: Jossey-Bass.

Schrock-Shenk, C. (1997), 'Spirituality: The Fertile Soil of Peacemaking', in Mennonite Conciliation Service, *Mediation and Facilitation Training Manual*, Akron, PA: Mennonite Conciliation Service, pp. 23–5.

Schwarz, R. (2002), *The Skilled Facilitator: A Comprehensive Resource for Consultants, Facilitators, Managers, Trainers, and Coaches*, San Francisco: Jossey-Bass.

Senge, Peter M. (2006), *The Fifth Discipline: The Art and Practice of the Learning Organization*, rev. edn, New York: Doubleday/Currency.

Sheal, P. R. (1989), *Staff Training Courses*, London: Kogan Page.

Shier-Jones, Angela (2005), *A Work in Progress: Methodists Doing Theology*, Werrington: Epworth.

Sibbet, D. (2010), *Visual Meetings: How Graphics, Sticky Notes and Idea Mapping Can Transform Group Productivity*, Hoboken, NJ: Wiley.

Sweet, L. I. (2000a), *Learn to Dance the Soul Salsa: 17 Surprising Steps for Godly Living in the 21st Century*, Grand Rapids, MI: Zondervan.

Sweet, L. I. (2000b), *Postmodern Pilgrims: First-century Passion for the 21st Century World*, Nashville, TN: Broadman & Holman.

Sweet, L. I. (2004), *Summoned to Lead*, Grand Rapids, MI: Zondervan.

Sweet, L. I., McLaren, B. D. and Haselmayer, J. (2003), *A is for Abductive: The Language of the Emerging Church*, Grand Rapids, MI: Zondervan.

Thompson, Neil (1998), *Promoting Equality: Challenging Discrimination and Oppression*, London: Macmillan.

Thompson, N. (2002), *People Skills*, 2nd edn, Basingstoke: Palgrave Macmillan.

Thompson, N. (2006), *People Problems*, Basingstoke: Palgrave Macmillan.

Thompson, N., Murphy, M. and Stradling, S. (1998), *Meeting the Stress Challenge*, Lyme Regis: Russell House.

Tuckman, B. W. (1965), 'Developmental Sequence in Small Groups', *Psychological Bulletin* 63:6, 384–99.

Bibliography

Vine, W. E. (1985), *An Expository Dictionary of New Testament Words*, Chicago: Moody Press.

Walton, A. (2012), *Dealing with Personal Criticism*, Cambridge: Grove.

Ward, F. (2005), *Lifelong Learning: Theological Education and Supervision*, London: SCM Press.

Wheatley, M. J. and Kellner-Rogers, M. (1996), *A Simpler Way*, San Francisco: Berrett-Koehler.

Whitehead, J. (2003), 'Integration and Incarnation: The Extent to Which Creative Training Methodologies Engender Deep Learning', unpublished MA dissertation, Sheffield University.

Whitney, D. and Trosten-Bloom, A. (2003), *The Power of Appreciative Inquiry*, San Francisco: Berrett-Koehler.

Widdicombe, C. (1994), *Group Meetings that Work*, Slough: St Paul's.

Woodward, J. and Pattison, S. (eds) (2000), *The Blackwell Reader in Pastoral and Practical Theology*, Oxford: Blackwell.

Further reading

Introduction and overview

Adair, J. (1993), *Effective Leadership*, London: Pan-Macmillan.

Heron, J. (1999), *The Complete Facilitator's Handbook*, London: Kogan Page.

Hogan, C. (2003), *Practical Facilitation: A Toolkit of Techniques*, London: Kogan Page.

Hunter, D., with Thorpe, S., Brown, H. and Bailey, A. (2007), *The Art of Facilitation: The Essentials for Leading Great Meetings and Creating Group Synergy*, rev. edn, San Francisco: Jossey-Bass.

1 Values and attributes of effective facilitators

Cloud, H. (2006), *Integrity: The Courage to Meet the Demands of Reality*, New York: HarperCollins.

Covey, S. (1989), *The Seven Habits of Highly Effective People*, London: Simon & Schuster.

Schwarz, R. (2002), *The Skilled Facilitator: A Comprehensive Resource for Consultants, Facilitators, Managers, Trainers, and Coaches*, San Francisco: Jossey-Bass.

2 Basic facilitation skills

Highmore Sims, N. (2006), *How to Run a Great Workshop: The Complete Guide to Designing and Running Brilliant Workshops and Meetings*, Harlow: Pearson.

Hogan, C. (2003), *Practical Facilitation: A Toolkit of Techniques*, London: Kogan Page.

Nash, S., Pimlott, J. and Nash, P. (2008), *Skills for Collaborative Ministry*, London: SPCK.

Thompson, N. (2002), *People Skills*, 2nd edn, Basingstoke: Palgrave Macmillan.

3 Culture setting: creating hospitable spaces

Cloud, H. and Townsend, J. (1992), *Boundaries*, Grand Rapids, MI: Zondervan.

Davis, M. (2002), *Walking on the Shore: A Way of Sharing Faith in Groups*, Chelmsford: Matthew James.

Inge, J. (2003), *A Christian Theology of Place*, Aldershot: Ashgate.

North, P. and North, J. (2007), *Sacred Space: House of God, Gate of Heaven*, London: Continuum.

4 Group stages, culture and roles

Belbin, R. M. (1981), *Management Teams: Why they Succeed or Fail*, Oxford: Butterworth-Heinemann.

Belbin, R. M. (1993), *Team Roles at Work*, Oxford: Butterworth-Heinemann.

Brown, R. (1988), *Group Processes: Dynamics Within and Between Groups*, Oxford, Blackwell.

Sibbett, D. (2011), *Visual Teams: Graphic Tools for Commitment, Innovation and High Performance*, Hoboken, NJ: Wiley.

5 Creative approaches to facilitation

Buzan, T. (2005), *The Ultimate Book of Mind Maps*, London: Thorsons.

Creaven, F. (2003), *Body and Soul: A Spirituality of Imaginative Creativity*, London: SPCK.

Fleming Drane, O. M. (2002), *Clowns, Storytellers, Disciples: Spirituality and Creativity for Today's Church*, Oxford: Bible Reading Fellowship.

Lucas, R. W. (2000), *The Big Book of Flip Charts: A Comprehensive Guide for Presenters, Trainers and Team Facilitators*, New York: McGraw Hill.

Silberman, M. and Lawson, K. (1995), *101 Ways to Make Training Active*, San Francisco: Jossey-Bass.

Whitney, D. and Trosten-Bloom, A. (2003), *The Power of Appreciative Inquiry*, San Francisco: Berrett-Koehler.

6 Conflict, criticism and effective interventions

Berne, E. (1964), *Games People Play: The Psychology of Human Relationships*, London: Penguin.

Goleman, D. (1996), *Emotional Intelligence: Why it can Matter more than IQ*, London: Bloomsbury.

Ringer, T. M. (2002), *Group Action: The Dynamics of Groups in Therapeutic, Educational and Corporate Settings*, London: Jessica Kingsley.

Runde, C. E. and Flanagan, T. A. (2008), *Building Conflict Competent Teams*, San Francisco: Jossey-Bass.

Thompson, N. (2006), *People Problems*, Basingstoke: Palgrave Macmillan.

7 Beginnings and endings

Carter, J. (2011), *Over 600 Icebreakers and Games*, Hope Books, <www.hopebooks.org>.

Wilson, P. and Long, I. (2008), *The Big Book of Blobs*, Milton Keynes: Speechmark.

8 Facilitating informal worship

Baker, J. (2010), *Curating Worship*, London: SPCK.

Earey, M. (2012), *Worship that Cares: An Introduction to Pastoral Liturgy*, London: SCM Press.

Ellis, C. (2009), *Approaching God: A Guide for Worship Leaders and Worshippers*, Norwich: Canterbury Press.

Kreider, A. and Kreider, E. (2009), *Worship and Mission After Christendom*, Milton Keynes: Paternoster.

9 Facilitating meetings

Peberdy, D. and Hammersley, J. (2009), *Brilliant Meetings: What to Know, Do and Say to have Fewer, Better Meetings*, Harlow: Pearson Education.

Sibbet, D. (2010), *Visual Meetings: How Graphics, Sticky Notes and Idea Mapping Can Transform Group Productivity*, Hoboken, NJ: Wiley.

10 Facilitating learning and reflection

Green, L. (1990), *Let's Do Theology: A Pastoral Cycle Resource Book*, London: Continuum.

Honey, P. and Mumford, A. (1992), *The Manual of Learning Styles*, Maidenhead: Peter Honey.

Jaques, D. (1991), *Learning in Groups*, London: Kogan Page.

Killen, P. O. and de Beer, J. (1994), *The Art of Theological Reflection*, New York: Crossroad.

LeFever, M. D. (1995), *Learning Styles: Reaching Everyone God Gave You to Teach*, Colorado Springs, CO: David C Cook.

Nash, S. and Nash, P. (2009), *Tools for Reflective Ministry*, London: SPCK.

Ward, F. (2005), *Lifelong Learning: Theological Education and Supervision*, London: SCM Press.

11 Facilitating decision-making processes

Brown, J. and Isaacs, D. (2005), *The World Café*, San Francisco: Berrett-Koehler.

Perkins, D. (2003), *King Arthur's Round Table: How Collaborative Conversations Create Smart Organizations*, Hoboken, NJ: Wiley.

12 Facilitating change

Bridges, W. (2009), *Managing Transitions*, 3rd edn, London: Nicholas Brearley.

Cameron, E. and Green, M. (2012), *Making Sense of Change Management*, London: Kogan Page.

Cormack, D. (1995), *Change Directions: New Ways Forward for Your Life, Your Church and Your Business*, Crowborough: Monarch.

Frost, M. and Hirsch, A. (2011), *The Faith of Leap: Embracing a Theology of Risk, Adventure and Courage*, Grand Rapids, MI: Baker Books.

Green, M. (2007), *Change Management Masterclass: A Step by Step Guide to Successful Change Management*, London: Kogan Page.

Index

Index